SOIL CARE FOR GARDENERS

GW00601995

SOIL CARE FOR GARDENERS

A Practical Guide

JIM MATHER

The Crowood Press

First published in 1988 by
The Crowood Press
Ramsbury, Marlborough,
Wiltshire SN8 2HE

British Library Cataloguing in Publication Data
Mather, Jim
Soil care.
1. Soils
I. Title
631.4

ISBN 1 85223 039 8

Line illustrations by Claire Upsdale-Jones

Typeset by Quorum Technical Services,
Cheltenham, Gloucestershire.
Printed in Great Britain by
Billing and Sons Ltd, Worcester

Contents

Introduction

In the lush, green land of Britain we take soil too much for granted. We neglect it and ill-treat it and then complain when plants we grow in it fail to reach a high standard (usually through our own failures). We forget that it is the 'good earth'.

When a new rose-bed was being made in my garden, and I was firming the roots and checking that the bushes had been set at the right depth, my helper, Buckie, waved a finger towards two or three and said, 'I had to put a bit more dirt around those.' Dirt! He meant soil of course, and good, clean soil at that. So why downgrade it by giving it that description? Perhaps it stemmed from boyhood scoldings for getting dirty when playing in the garden.

He was referring specifically to basic soil dug from the spare patch, as distinct from the enriched soil we called the 'planting mixture'. This mixture was made up of good soil, moist peat, and a sprinkling of bone-meal. We had worked liberal quantities of it among the roots, and had used up all that we had prepared. Buckie knew his soil and how to treat it, and that was why he wanted to point out that he had used a couple of spades full of unfortified soil to finish the planting.

What that little episode does, I hope, is to remind you that soil is a complex and interesting subject, worth knowing more about. This book sets out to explore those complexities in a practical way (down to earth, if you will forgive the pun) and to help you get the best out of your lawns, flower borders, and fruit and vegetable patches.

Much of the surface of the planet earth is covered with soil, which we know also as earth. But large areas of that surface are not suitable for cultivation, being covered by water, rocks, icy mountains, or burning sands. Writing as a gardener, and not as a Master of Science, I refer to the earth's crust as 'soil' because all of it – including the bottom of the sea – either is, or could become, capable of supporting vegetable or animal life, given the right temperatures and other elements.

It has taken nature many millions of years to transform various parts of the earth's surface into ground which man's comparatively puny efforts could make habitable and cultivable, or, if you like, to give us our soil. We use or abuse it in many ways. We cover it with buildings, bury it under concrete to make roads, dump rubbish on it, plant trees in it, play games on it and curse it or bless it. Above all, we rely on it for our food. Yet in all this we rarely stop to consider exactly what soil is. In this book, we are considering garden soil, which means that depth to which we can reach with a spade, plus those strata which significantly influence its behaviour. Our interest in garden soil is mainly concerned with how to get the best out of cultivating it.

To the geologist, the soil is a crust several yards deep, going down to what he calls bedrock; whilst to the gardener, soil is the shallower layer in which plants grow, consisting of crumbs of rock, mixed with organic matter from decomposed plant and animal remains. Such soil is a living thing, not some inert dirt. It is full of micro-organisms and animal life mostly too small to see, besides the worms and grubs that are big enough to be noticed.

In the bit of earth we call garden, we naturally tend not to think of all this. We expect the ground under our feet to yield easily to the spade so that we can dig planting holes and make plants grow in it. If it is unyielding, or if our plants do badly, we ask what is wrong with the soil and what can be added to it to make it satisfy our wants. This is rather like seeking an ointment to clear spots without trying to find their cause. The spots will go, but will keep coming back, and eventually the ointment may cease to be effective. Similarly, quick spot treatment, like feeding or watering, may solve a problem concerning plant performance, but will not tell us why the problem arose or how to avoid it by proper assessment of the condition and by longer-term corrective action.

The following chapters should help you to avoid that sort of mistake by showing how soils differ and by guiding you towards simple answers which will ensure first-class results with whatever is grown in the garden.

1
The Earth's Crust

In his famous *Dictionary of the English Language*, Dr Samuel Johnson defines crust as 'any external shell; ... an encrustation or collection of matter into a hard body'. That second definition not only describes many of the rocky mountains of the earth but points to the process by which the crust was created.

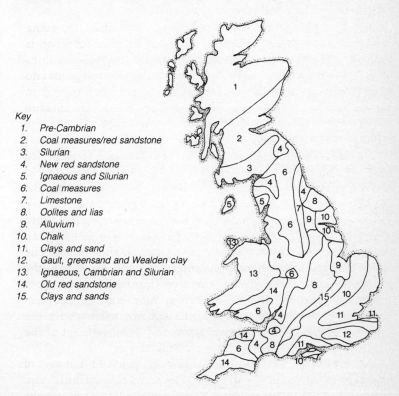

Key
1. Pre-Cambrian
2. Coal measures/red sandstone
3. Silurian
4. New red sandstone
5. Ignaeous and Silurian
6. Coal measures
7. Limestone
8. Oolites and lias
9. Alluvium
10. Chalk
11. Clays and sand
12. Gault, greensand and Wealden clay
13. Ignaeous, Cambrian and Silurian
14. Old red sandstone
15. Clays and sands

Fig 1   British soil types.

Scientists can take us back 600 million years to a time when the earth was a gas, which first changed to liquid and then formed a crust. That crust itself has changed in almost every way, including shape, over the years since. The relative areas of sea and land masses were unstable, and for millions of years they kept changing their shapes and contours. Earthquakes had a big influence in creating the varying land formations which exist in Britain today, and on the differences in surface soils. Quakes twisted and buckled the different geological layers, throwing to the surface various strata – limestone in Yorkshire; chalk on the North and South Downs; gravel, greensand and clay in different areas of the London Basin and the Thames Valley.

Next came the ice ages, with massive glaciers carving out V-shaped valleys and grinding the rock off hills and mountains to produce what later became sediment found under the melted ice. It was not until about 10,000 years ago that the last of several ice ages began to pass. Melting ice raised the sea-level until more and more land was covered, and Britain became separated from the European continent by sea.

Plant and animal life had existed long before this, and had undergone frequent modification by evolution, much of it influenced by the major climatic changes. Indeed it is estimated to be 300 million years since peat and coal seams formed from swamped forests.

BEGINNINGS

The melting of the ice 10,000 years ago and the subsequent arrival of warmer summers began the gradual process of improving conditions which inspired man to attempt the cultivation of the soil and the taming of animals.

With the ice out of the way, the sun was able to heat the rocks, causing expansion and contraction. This caused the rocks to split into smaller and smaller pieces and helped to produce sand and silt. Vegetation added the decaying matter to mix with the sand, silt, clay and grit to produce cultivable soil.

It was about 7,000 years ago that the world saw the beginnings of agriculture and the domestication of animals. Not surprisingly, valley areas were chosen as the earliest sites, the presence of soil moisture being a critical factor in the choice, but not the only factor. The soil in the valleys was made up of small particles washed down from the heights and offered the best hope for cultivation, bearing in mind that at first, man had only his hands and feet with which to work the soil. For hunting, primitive man relied on his bare hands – and his cunning – to catch and kill his prey. As his ambitions grew, so did his resourcefulness, and he fashioned tools from wood to help him catch larger prey.

These early hunting sticks were probably also the first tools used for cultivation. Change of usage brings change of design, and the shape, size and weight of the pieces of wood had to be modified to meet different uses. Improvement in tools meant improvement in cultivation, which widened the scope of land available to work, and in turn called for better tools to help increase the cultivations.

As each settlement prospered, it attracted the attention of others and kindled a desire in man to defend himself and his possessions. Hence the tool designed for the soil became a weapon, and the interchange of ideas for hunting, fighting, and tilling led to many variations in design and material – eventually taking in flints and ultimately iron.

CULTIVABLE SOIL

As tools improved it became possible to cultivate stronger, heavier soil and so cultivation moved up out of the valleys. There it was soon discovered that soil is affected by climate and by exposure to weather, but it was many years before it was realised that several other factors influenced the soil and its performance. These include direction of slope, height in relation to adjoining land and to sea-level, degree and direction of slope, direction of prevailing wind, and anything that affects weather – such as latitude and distance from the sea.

Cultivable soil, as distinct from the hard rock from which it originated (and that includes volcanic rock), is unstable to a certain degree. It has to be, being full of living organisms and a mixture of particles which vary in their reaction to the elements.

3

For example, fibres swell when wetted and shrink when dry, while flinty particles reject water. Heavy rain can move any soil particle – indeed water is a powerful force – and steeply sloping ground is vulnerable to severe disturbance by a heavy downpour.

Water Erosion

Farmers try to keep cultivations to a minimum on sloping ground, especially where the slope is fairly steep, to protect the surface from heavy rains. A major example of how cultivation affects sloping ground in heavy rain has been seen in Bangladesh in recent years. Massive deforestation in the foothills of the Himalayas is the root cause of devastating floods there.

Trees, with their large root systems not only consume a large amount of water, but also hold it and slow its movement. The rain takes a long time to soak into the root-filled soil and makes a steady, continuous trickle into streams and rivers. When the trees have been removed, the rain-water rushes downhill, mostly on the surface, filling streams and rivers so rapidly that they flood.

Floods are not the only disastrous consequences of deforestation. In South America, it rendered vast areas barren and useless for cultivation after the failure of a scheme that was intended to do the opposite. Millions of dollars were spent on deforestation, with the aim of opening up the ground for food crops. The subsequent flooding washed away the topsoil. Incidentally, a further factor is that forests are essential to maintain the balance between oxygen and carbon dioxide, and when substantial areas of forest are cut down, this balance is upset.

For the farmer or gardener, an ideal way to deal with a steep slope is to keep the ground grassed down, as this involves no soil disturbance, but it is not practical as a permanent answer. Where a slope has to be cultivated, the good farmer practises what is known as 'contour ploughing', which means that the furrows run across the slope. This minimises the erosion caused when heavy rain comes soon after such cultivation; there will simply be a little spilling over from furrow to furrow. But if the land is ploughed up and down the slope, heavy rain can rush

4

Fig 2   Contour ploughing.

down the furrows carrying valuable topsoil down and out into the roadway at the foot.

Gardeners should note this when growing vegetables in rows, and should conserve their soil by running the rows across the slope where possible, rather than up and down. For more permanent planting on a fairly steep slope, you could try terracing, which involves chopping out wide, level beds (terraces) with steep steps between them. Permanent planting is of course a help towards control of water erosion. Where the slope is not steep, regular mulching with light, bulky material such as peat, leaf-mould, bark chippings, or straw will cushion the surface against heavy rain and also slow down the movement of surface water.

Direction of Slope

The direction in which a slope faces will have a major influence on the soil and its performance, independent of the water effects. A southerly slope traps a great deal of the sun's heat, and this is generally helpful to plant growth. To make the most

5

before

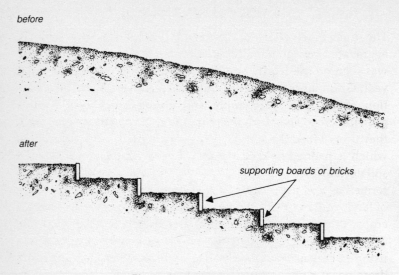

after

supporting boards or bricks

Fig 3   Terracing on a slope.

of this extra warmth, care should be taken to limit overheating and drying out of the soil – this can be done by mulching as before. Without such protection in a hot spell, light soil could go dust-dry and some of it could be carried away by the wind. Heavy soil is also affected by exposure to hot sun, which causes it to crack open. Any roots in such soil would then be left open to the air, and suffer serious damage. On a south-facing slope, with rows running across the slope as previously suggested, the plants in the rows would give some shade to the soil, thus limiting the risk of wind erosion. The soil erosion caused by the combined effect of the sun creating a surface dust, followed by winds blowing away such a surface, can become infinitely worse in a period of prolonged drought. In fact this combination can, and does, create deserts, particularly in extremely hot climates.

Another soil-damaging factor, even in gardens where the soil is well cared for, will be seen when a prolonged drought is broken by extremely heavy rain. The rain falling faster than the ground can soak it up will stir the surface soil, wash it around, and carry some into the gutters. Surface mulching before the rain comes will help cope with such situations.

Causes of Dust-Bowls

The dust-bowl effect of heat and drought can be severely aggravated by some methods of fertiliser use. Evidence of this was seen on the North American continent in one bad drought year. Granular or powdered chemical fertilisers have the attraction of being easy to apply and giving quick results on a growing crop. They feed the crop, but their disadvantage is that they do not feed the soil. They do not supply the bulky material which is needed to keep the soil alive, with the result that the soil deteriorates into dust. The great American dust-bowls were formed as a direct result of this method of farming – large areas of land, well fed by chemical fertilisers, were unable to support crops. Why such chemicals are not enough for the soil will be discussed further at a later stage, but meanwhile note that when using chemical fertiliser you can help the soil by applying a dressing of compost-forming materials – such as peat – at the same time.

Shade

One drawback in the practice of putting crop-rows across a south-facing slope to keep in harmony with the contours, is that one side of the row is in permanent shade, whereas the popular policy of running the row from north to south ensures that sun reaches both sides. It also restricts the planting of tall subjects such as runner beans, because the rows would have to be some distance apart to avoid being completely shaded by their neighbours. Even so, this method is still better than encouraging soil erosion.

Ground which slopes down to the north does not get the same benefit from the sun as does a south-facing slope. It is slower to warm up and will not reach a temperature sufficient for growth until later in the year. This is known as late ground, and does not create any major problem, provided that the slope is not too steep. However, such ground is commercially better for a late-maturing crop such as maincrop potatoes, than for an early-season crop like strawberries.

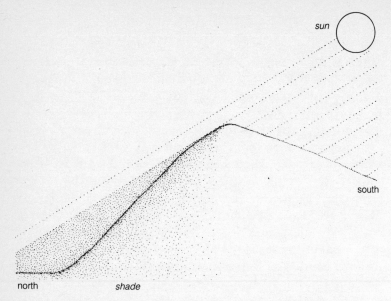

Fig 4   *The effect of slope on heat retention. The northern
slope receives little heat when the sun is low in the sky. The
southern slope is exposed to more sun and therefore warms
up early in the season and retains more heat. The angle of
the sun's rays encourages penetration.*

FROSTY VALLEYS

Water is not the only element that flows downhill, sometimes
with undesirable results. One of the unexpected blessings
discovered by the earliest venturers out of the valleys on to
higher ground was that they escaped the radiation frosts of late
spring. There are still people who expect valleys to be always
warm, but the fact is that cold air, like water, flows downhill.
Warm air, being lighter than cold, rises in a pattern of convec-
tion and colder air curves down to replace it.

After a fine, sunny day with no cloud to interrupt the air flow,
the frosty air runs down like a stream to the lowest spots, which
consequently are termed frost pockets. A hedge across a slope
can interrupt this down-flow so that frost pockets occur on the
high side of such hedges as well as at the bottom of the slope.
Fruit blossoms and tender plants can be killed by spring frost

8

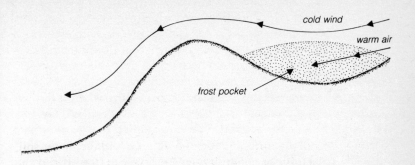

Fig 5   Spring frost. Warm air is trapped in the frost pocket.
The warm air rises and in a cloudless sky can rise into the
frosty layer before curving downwards to force down the
cold air layer which causes ground frost.

and vulnerable plants should not be planted in frost pockets, or
not planted out at all until the spring frosts finish, at the end of
May or early June. Early-flowering subjects such as camellia
should avoid not only frost pockets but also early-morning sun.
When the flower-buds are caught by overnight frost, the quick
thaw brought about by early sun will damage them because

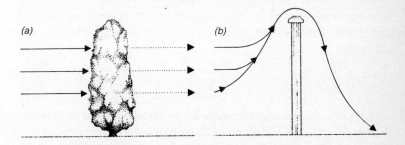

Fig 6   Effects of hedge and fence on wind turbulence.
(a) Wind passes through a hedge which offers little resistance
and so causes little wind turbulence, which is beneficial to
both soil and plants. (b) Wind bounces over a solid fence or
wall, creating turbulence on the other side as the wind hits
the ground. Turbulence could be avoided by using an
open-work fence which would allow the wind to filter
through.

frozen fibres can break when the temperature jumps up suddenly. If planted in the shade, where the air warms slowly, they can escape damage.

Strategically planted hedges can divert the flow of cold air down a slope and funnel it to where it will do no harm – into a road for instance, but not on to a neighbour's land.

Wind is a lateral air flow that can be damaging when it flows in strength, but hedges or fences can be used effectively to protect plants and soil from it. The easiest mistake is to assume that a strong, solid fence is a more effective barrier than a hedge – it isn't. The wind will bounce over the top and, coming down a few feet further on, will whip up dry soil into a dust-cloud. A hedge will let the wind through, but will filter it and reduce its force. One of the main fascinations of soil is that it varies so much from region to region and even from garden to garden, as to make it a popular subject of conversation. For varying reasons, we all want to improve the quality of whatever soil comes under our influence. The farmer wants mainly to know how he can make it produce an abundance of good crops or of grass to feed animals. The town-dweller wants mainly to use it to beautify his surroundings or help his recreation.

But the farmer is certainly not without an eye for beautiful surroundings or for the chances of recreation; and the town-dweller is aware of the soil's importance in food production. So clearly we all have a common interest in improving and maintaining the soil. Our reasons for tilling it vary, and consequently our types of cultivations vary also, showing wide differences in demands, methods and results. For example, once an area of parkland is put down to grass, it needs no more digging until the design has to be changed. But if an area is to grow potatoes it needs digging more than once a year and the soil will need feeding to replenish the plant foods lost to the potatoes. Furthermore, other factors will then affect the soil, such as a build-up of diseases and pests which will make it essential to switch from potatoes to some other crop.

2

Assessment

When you move house and survey the garden, the temptation is to make hurried decisions on how to change the general layout to suit your ideas of how it should look. This will lead you quickly to thoughts of plant changes – some plants you will want to discard because they don't appeal to you; others you will want to move to make way for fresh subjects. The aim is commendable, indeed it is refreshing and exciting to think of stamping your personality on your garden as quickly as possible. However, if you act too hastily in putting your ideas into effect, regardless of soil factors, it can be like hurrying on to a railway station and leaping on to a departing train without checking that it is the one you want. It can be a mistake, and a difficult one to correct. Adapting an old adage, you should remember that those who act in haste will repent at leisure.

After your first casual look at the general layout, take a closer look at the plants, considering them in groups and also individually as seen from different angles. The view from the kitchen window can be more important than that from a bedroom window. A tree or shrub may be there for its beauty or just to screen an unsightly spot. Before you move it you should consider why it was selected, what you would like in its place, and whether the site and soil would suit your proposed replacement.

CLUE PLANTS

Some guide to the state of your soil can be gathered from the plants and the quality of their growth, but your garden may not be typical of the neighbourhood, so look beyond your boundary fence to see what grows well in the surrounding plots.

11

Fig 7   Large elm and root system.

There are plenty of reasons why the decline in the elm tree population is to be regretted, including the knowledge that where a big elm is seen to be thriving, it is safe to assume that the soil must be good. You are not likely to have – or want – a big old elm in your garden, but look around at trees nearby. Perhaps you are not sure whether you can recognise an elm in winter when the leaves are off, but there are other easily recognised signs of soil fertility. For instance, where hawthorns and nettles thrive, you can be satisfied that the soil is reasonable. Chickweed, groundsel and sowthistle also suggest good, fertile soil. Fruit growers looking for new areas to plant are always happy when they see nettles looking healthy and strong – they say that soil which grows nettles will grow good fruit.

Where you see rushes doing well, you can guess that the ground is too damp for general gardening. The presence of moss, slimy growth and sedges will confirm that drainage needs improving. To seek more specific clues regarding the character of your soil, look out for heather, camellia and rhododendron (including azalea). Where they grow well the soil is inclined to be acidic rather than chalky. If the rhododendrons look tired and have yellowing leaves, you can suspect that the soil is alkaline (chalky or limy). Large patches of clover could be another indication of the presence of lime.

Lawns do not give as good a clue to the state of the soil as many people expect. The presence of moss is sometimes put down to acidity and sometimes to bad drainage, but in fact the trouble is more often due to hunger or to excessively short mowing. The poor general state of a lawn is mainly caused by the gardener's shortcomings rather than the soil's lack of potential; while a beautiful, rich lawn may owe more to good feeding and good management than to the basic quality of the soil.

DRAINAGE

Drainage is a likely cause of the trouble when lawn moss fails to respond to routine moss-control treatment, but it is wise to look at the general state of the garden's drainage and not just at the lawn in particular. A simple check on drainage can be made by first digging a hole about 2ft(60cm) square and 2ft(60cm) deep. There should be no water settling in the hole unless you have dug during a spell of wet weather – in normal conditions it should be reasonably dry when you finish digging it. The test is then to fill it from the hose and see how long the water takes to disappear. If it drains away almost as fast as you run it in, then your problem is not one of how to improve drainage but how to improve your soil's capacity for water retention. Assuming the hole fills up, leave it for an hour. After that time, if water remains in the hole, the drainage is inadequate. Whether or not that problem is significant enough to call for action will depend on what depth of water is still standing and how much longer it takes to drain completely. (You will find advice on both drainage and moisture retention in the following chapter.)

13

SOIL TYPES

The next step in garden assessment is to handle the soil and take a closer look at its physical make-up. A word of warning here: be careful to take precautions against tetanus (lockjaw). The bacteria which cause this disease come from horses, surviving for long periods in the soil where horses work or graze, or where stable manure has been used. Ideally, all who do any gardening should be inoculated against the disease, and the inoculation should be 'topped up' regularly. Wounds or scratches can become infected, so these must be treated, and it is wise also to wear strong gloves when gardening.

Presuming you have seen to all this, now pick up a handful of soil and rub it between your fingers. If it feels gritty, try to grip it into a ball, making sure it is not dust-dry. Sand will crumble away and not make a ball. Varying proportions of sand and loam in the ball of soil will indicate whether it is what is termed a loamy sand or sandy loam, the latter being a useful soil, and generally popular because it is easy to cultivate. Loam is generally accepted as the most important physical constituent of a good soil. It is broadly defined as the near-surface soil, which contains fibrous matter including roots and leaf-mould.

Continuing with the squeeze test, if the soil makes a slightly sticky ball, with a kind of soapy feeling, and can be pulled apart easily, it is basically silt; and if it is a sticky ball which is difficult to pull apart, it is basically clay. Varying results when you try to break the ball will tell you whether or not it has a high loam content. Soil with a high proportion of loam has excellent potential for cultivation, whether it is clay loam, sandy loam or silt loam. Clay is the best of these, but it should also have sufficient sandy or gritty elements to keep it from binding (like the sticky ball).

Problem Soils

The three categories of soil least helpful to the gardener are those which are extremely stony, sandy, or peaty and boggy. But it is only the extremes that cause worry, as soils which are only slightly too stony, sandy or peaty can be easily modified to give satisfactory results. Stony soils, light soils (sandy loam and loamy sand), and medium soils (medium loam and silt loam), will need peat, leaf-mould or some other source of extra fibre, in varying quantities depending on how stony, how sandy and so on. Heavy soils (clay, clay loam, and sandy clay) may need more drainage. Details on how to help your soil by these and other physical means are given in the next chapter, but it is up to you to first make a reasonable assessment of the proportions of clay, sand, loam and other elements present, to help determine what quantities of additives are needed. The soil's chemical needs will also be influenced by this assessment, especially where chalky (lime) soils are concerned – such soils will be considered under the broad heading of chemical rather than physical qualities (*see* Chapter 4). Doubtless the garden in general has an important influence on the choice when you are buying a house, but the nature of the soil will not be an important factor unless there is a particular reason for wanting a specific soil. That is to say, the specialist who intends to fill the garden with an acid-loving subject such as camellia would avoid a chalky soil; but generally the house-buyer is concerned with a dozen other factors and is ready to accept whatever type of soil it stands on. This will mean choosing the plants to fit the garden rather than choosing a garden to suit the plants. This is not usually as severely limiting a factor as is sometimes suggested, and where it is, the choice of good plants is still an ample one. Nevertheless, it is a mistake to disregard completely either the nature of the soil or any other of the various characteristics of the garden when choosing the plants.

Supreme optimists just plant whatever they are fond of. Some people who consider themselves more careful will dig the odd spade full of soil and examine it – if they like the feel of it they will pronounce it good, then proceed to plant what they like. In all these cases, disappointments are inevitable, and if you feel like copying such ideas I suggest you resist the temptation to plant anything expensive during the first season.

SOIL-TEST KITS

There is no need to be pessimistic and reject plants just because a neighbour says they don't suit the soil. You could well find that the soil is more friendly than you have been led to expect, and that the neighbour's experience is due to some other factor. It is wise to buy a small soil-test kit to help you find out the pH value of your soil before finalising your list of plants. This pH (which stands for potential of hydrogen) is the unit of measurement of acidity or alkalinity, and is probably the most critical soil factor to consider. Alkaline soil has a high potential of hydrogen, whilst acid soil has a low pH value.

Even so, it must be emphasised once more that you should not be unduly alarmed if your garden is inclined either to acidity or alkalinity, as only the extremes will create problems. For the average gardener, knowing the soil's pH will stop the risk of his struggling with plants which would be too unhappy, and help him to make small adjustments so that plants may give their best. While it is hardly practical to convert the soil from one pH extreme to the other, it is easy to give a lime-lover a little extra lime or an acid-lover a little sulphur or other helpful soil treatment.

It is impossible to convert a whole garden from one soil extreme to the other, although there are various methods which can be used to improve the situation. For example, a garden on

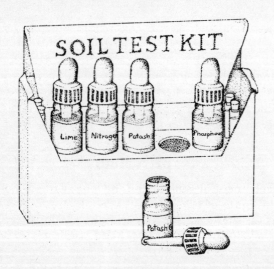

Fig 8   A soil-test kit is essential to any gardener.

chalk land will have alkaline soil, and if you plant rhododendrons on such land they will not flourish unless the soil is treated with sufficient acidifier. No such treatment is really practical because it will not bring permanent change, but if you were determined to grow a small group of rhododendrons, you could create a small, raised island of slightly acid soil, as explained later, which would keep them happy if given regular treatment.

To describe plants as lime-haters is sometimes as unkind as saying that an asthma sufferer is a flower-hater. Most people with asthma love flowers but are too sensitive to the pollen in certain conditions. Similarly, those plants which do not tolerate lime happily are upset by chlorosis, which is mainly caused by an excess of lime. The disease can have other causes, however, thus the cure may not simply be a matter of getting rid of alkalinity.

Chlorosis is a condition which manifests itself in a shortage of chlorophyll, the matter which gives the green colouring to leaves and stems when they are exposed to light – affected leaves go yellow or even white. Chlorophyll is not just a colouring matter, however, but an essential agent for plant growth. It picks up certain rays from the spectrum of sunlight (the red, yellow, green, blue and violet) to give the plant the energy with which to break down carbon dioxide and water and help the formation of sugars and starches. An excess of lime in the soil locks up minerals essential to the production of chlorophyll, such as iron, and the effect is termed 'lime-induced chlorosis'. At the other extreme, a soil lacking in calcium will be over-acidic and sour, and this condition will lock up manganese and other nutrients.

pH Values

A precisely neutral soil would be one with a potential of hydrogen figure of seven (written as pH7). A rating of pH7.5 indicates a slight alkalinity, with higher figures denoting stronger alkalinity. A rating of pH6.5 indicates only a slight acidity, and most garden plants will grow well in such a soil. From pH6 downwards, the readings indicate stronger degrees of acidity, with a value of pH4.5 representing extreme acidity.

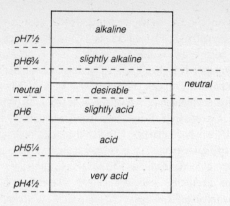

Fig 9   Scale of soil acidity. Proprietary soil-test kits usually indicate acidity ranges as shown in this diagram, e.g. 6–6¾, 6¾–7, and so on. Neutral lies at about 7pH. Slightly below means a little acidity, and slightly above indicates a little alkalinity. The slightly acid reading of 6½ makes a good average for most garden plants.

Soil-test outfits suitable for small gardens are available from shops and garden centres. They will help you calculate the soil's main fertiliser needs, as well as showing you its pH rating, by a few simple tests. Soil in small test-tubes is treated with solutions which change colour according to the strength of fertiliser elements in the sample, and according to its pH. Colour charts make it easy to match your readings to colours and thus find what quantities of nutrients or pH correctives should be needed.

With such an outfit you may be able to get a check-list of the range of pH values applicable to a list of popular garden subjects and house-plants. The list will then help you decide whether your soil suits the plants which you wish to grow.

Analysing Samples

The most frequent mistake made in do-it-yourself soil testing is faulty sampling, and the next most common mistake is not making enough tests. A proper sample of about a spoonful of soil should be taken, with clean equipment, from about 4in(10cm) below the surface. Use a series of sampling points in order to cover all parts of the garden. Taking two or three samples from each sampling point is advisable, to enable cross-checking and avoid rogue answers. Care should be taken to keep each sample separate from the rest and properly labelled. Some people mix two or three samples from one point but this is not helpful. Crumble the sample by breaking it with a spoon, and discard small flints. Carefully follow the directions given on the package, especially those concerning the cleanliness of equipment.

One complication which you must not ignore is that the soil will not have a completely stable pH value. In an industrial area, fumes from factories may increase its acidity, as might car exhaust fumes and other atmospheric conditions in built-up areas. Regular additions of peat may increase acidity, while compost which is rich in nitrogen may surprise you by increasing in alkalinity. Even the plants themselves affect the soil over the years. This means that if you are doing any planting where the soil pH is a critical factor, you must not rely on records which are two years old or older.

When making your soil test, you should divide the garden into sections and have more than one test spot in each section. Do not simply divide it geometrically, but separate areas of heavy shade from those in full sun, areas which receive sun early in the day from those which do not get sun until later, higher ground from lower ground, south-facing slopes from north-facing slopes, and exposed sections from sheltered sections.

Some sections will qualify for more than one of these categories, and if so all the details should be noted in your soil-test record. For instance, one north-sloping section may be in heavy shade and sheltered, while another north-sloping section may be in full sun and exposed. No single feature is enough to indicate how well any particular subject will grow, but the influence of each will soon become obvious if you try making two sowings or plantings of the same subject at the same time in different parts of the garden. Plants which like warm, sunny conditions will be slow even on a sunny patch if the ground slopes down to the north, but will thrive on ground sloping to the south.

An interesting anecdote on that concerns the late Earl Lloyd George, the famous statesman, who loved the soil and was a keen plantsman. Coming from North Wales he was deeply conscious of the need to avoid any site shut in by mountains. When he was offered his first piece of land at Churt, in Surrey, which he later expanded into a large agricultural estate, he wanted to be assured that he could build a house with a good view there.

The land offer came to him by long-distance telephone from his secretary Frances Stevenson (whom he subsequently married). A decision was urgent because another bidder was about to buy it. Lloyd George asked for full details about the lie of the land. He wanted to know in which direction the ground sloped away from the summit where he wanted to build his house. When Frances told him she thought it sloped to the south, he was delighted and promptly told her he would call it 'Bron-y-de'. Freely translated from the Welsh, 'Bron-y-de' indicates a breast of ground with a south-facing slope. A compass check soon proved that in fact it sloped to the west, but Lloyd George stuck to the name. As he acquired more acres of land, 'Bron-y-de' was adopted as the name of the estate. The estate was broken up after Lloyd George's death. I later bought a small part of it, including a house built by Lloyd George.

The story is a reminder that the direction of slope is a factor of concern to every farmer and gardener. For instance, a summer crop like strawberries would miss the early (top price) market if grown on a north slope; early potatoes should be grown on a warm south slope, while lates might have to go on a cooler slope.

WHICH PLANTS WILL GROW?

The kind of question most frequently asked is, 'Will it be all right for xyz?', and 'What must I do to help it grow my xyz?' Substitute the name of your own pet plant or plant group for the xyz and you will bring the problem home to yourself. This will help you appreciate that getting the best from your soil needs some careful thought. But the effort is well worth while because it makes the difference between a mediocre garden and an attractive one; between a plant which just struggles on and one which grows well and sparkles.

The chief limiting factor is the degree of acidity or alkalinity (the pH level) of the soil, because this is where the plant itself is least able to adjust. So after your soil test, it is advisable to sort out your plants according to soil preference. After that you should try to match up each plant with the other characteristics of the spot where you want to grow it. For example, the popular subject broom (*Cytisus*), likes an acid soil (pH 5 to pH6). But simply giving it an acid soil is not enough, because in siting it you might note that it likes a dry spot, in full sun, and is happy in a seaside atmosphere.

It cannot be emphasised too often that by far the majority of permanent plants in the gardens of Britain grow happily in a soil that is neutral or slightly acid. Most gardens have soil which fits into those categories, and where the soil is extremely acid or extremely alkaline, the fact is well known locally – and usually beyond. If you were looking over a piece of new ground you would almost certainly be told of any such extreme. Therefore, in planning and planting, your main concern should be just to avoid those plants which really are extremely sensitive about a soil pH slightly above or below neutral, until you have had time to do the necessary testing. If you knew the ground to be chalky, you could get on and plant broom, but you would have to save the rhododendrons until you could find a way of giving their roots a more hospitable soil. Such adjustment is possible, but it is certainly not simple – gardeners with chalky soils look upon the cultivation of plants which are over-sensitive to lime as a great challenge.

Raised Beds

The best way to attempt a permanent adjustment is to make an island bed of peaty soil, treated to lower its pH severely. This must be a raised bed, because a bed on the flat would be influenced too easily by the surrounding soil, and would quickly revert. Various compounds, mostly based on aluminium sulphate, are available for lowering the soil pH to help it nourish acid-loving plants. These must not be applied indiscriminately but must be given in measured doses according to the results of your soil test. Using sulphate of ammonia as a nitrogen fertiliser has an acidifying effect, and this should be kept in mind when other treatments are being given.

Perhaps the simplest treatment to convert a patch wanted for planting acid-lovers is common flowers of sulphur. If you have

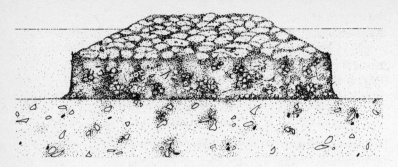

*Fig 10   A raised bed can be of benefit where soil is poor.
Some form of support, such as planks or old railway sleepers
can be a good idea.*

a chalky soil, try lacing it well with peat, building it into a raised
bed, and stirring in flowers of sulphur in quantities indicated by
your soil test – 1lb(0.45kg) to every 4 square yards (3.3m²) would
reduce a chalky pH of 7.5 or 8 to a slightly acid level of 6.5 in one
season.

Following this basic treatment it is essential to make regular
soil checks so that signs of loss of acidity can be detected and
promptly corrected. In practice, experienced gardeners find that
the plants themselves will give sufficient indication that more
treatment is needed, by poorer growth or a lack of lustre. In such
cases watering with sequestrene preparations is a popular practice. Some enthusiasts, having created raised island beds of
sulphur-treated soil, will top up with an annual dose of
sequestrenes.

Unlocking Minerals

Where such drastic treatment as the creation of special beds is
not necessary, but where the soil is just not quite acidic enough
for acid-loving plants, the sequestrene treatment alone is usually
enough. Sequestrenes rely on sequestrol which is a chelating
agent whose function is to protect metallic elements from the
action of calcium in the soil. This ensures that these trace
elements do not get locked up and made unavailable to the plant.

Where the soil is acid, the task of making it fit for plants which
like alkaline soils is quite straightforward. A soil test will tell you

the degree of acidity and the amount of liming needed to correct it. Allow as long an interval as possible – a minimum of six weeks – between liming and manuring. Lime reacts on the nitrogen and releases it in the form of ammonia gas. Ideally, lime in spring after manuring in autumn.

Acid Rain

Soil tends to become more acid naturally under cultivation, and farmers used to apply lime regularly, especially when there was a government subsidy to help pay for it. Perhaps this liming disguised the fact that acid rain was falling on the land – certainly acid rain was not much spoken of until recent years, after the lime application fell dramatically. Acid rain is caused by industrial fumes which rise into the cloud layer, are absorbed by the cloud moisture, and are carried across seas and continents by the wind, to fall far away from the source of the acidity.

Its prolonged effect has caused a good deal of political controversy and has intensified efforts to filter fumes more thoroughly before discharging them into the atmosphere. Only remote regions seem to have had the soil contaminated, and not gardens in towns or villages. But where you do suspect that your soil may have been affected, a normal soil test should indicate it and liming will probably correct it fairly quickly.

SHRUBS FOR ACID SOILS

To enable you to choose shrubs which will be happy in your soil, a few suggestions are listed, beginning with plants which do not like lime.

Andromeda
Azalea
Calluna
Camellia
Clethra
Erica (summer flowerers)
Fothergilla species

Gaulteria
Kalmia species
Pernettya (Prickly Heath)
Pieris
Rhododendron

SHRUBS FOR ALKALINE SOILS

There are shrubs which will thrive in a moderately limey soil, are happy in a neutral soil, and will tolerate soil slightly on the acid side of neutral. Because these do not thrive in acid soil some people class them as plants for alkaline soils. This is restrictive and somewhat misleading, and I feel that they are better listed as neutral. In my own records, I have always classed them as 'suitable for ordinary garden soil', though that may seem a little vague.

The shrubs in the following list for alkaline soils are those which my experience suggests are at their happiest and best in such an environment. There is always room for other opinions, but if you plant any of these on chalky ground, at least they will not let you down.

Berberis
Buddleia
Cytisus (Broom)
Fagus sylvatica (good hedging)
Genista (another Broom)
Hebe
Hypericum
Lavendula
Paeonia (tree species)
Physocarpus
Potentilla
Prunus
Rosmarinus
Senecio
Syringa
Weigela

With herbaceous plants – annuals, biennials and perennials – pH is not so critical as to restrict or limit planting plans. It is accepted that lily of the valley prefers an acid soil and wallflower prefers an alkaline one, but many gardens can support them both comfortably. Again, watch herbaceous plants for signs that they are not happy. Wallflowers, for instance, are subject to the club root fungus which sometimes afflicts brassicas on acid soils. The same remedy applies – clear them out, lime the soil, and do not repeat the crop on the same site.

ROTATION PLANS

In the vegetable garden too, the pH factor is not critical if proper care is taken with crop groupings and rotation. The main purposes of crop rotation are to get the best out of the soil, by

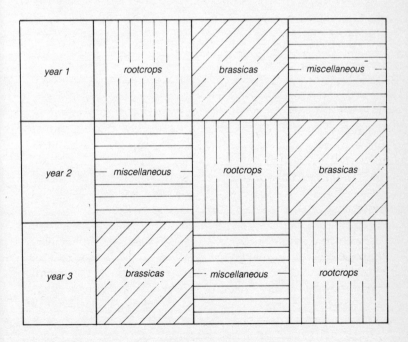

Fig 11   Simple crop rotation plan (3-year).

letting each group of plants take its share of its preferred nutrients; and limiting the scope of pests seeking permanent hosts. But an important effect of the process is also to prevent the build-up of acidity or alkalinity which comes with mono-cropping. For a three-year rotation in the vegetable garden the plant groupings are rootcrops, brassicas, and miscellaneous crops (such as peas, beans and onions). The garden is divided into three plots, one for each group. Plot 2, for the brassicas, is limed – normally this is done without any soil test, a pH of up to 7.5 being acceptable.

For the following year, the rootcrops move up from plot 2 to plot 3; and the miscellaneous crops move around to plot 1. This time, the lime goes on plot 3 for the brassicas. The same pattern of rotation continues in the following years – the crop in plot 1 moves to plot 2; plot 2's crop moves up to plot 3; and the final crop moves on from plot 3 to plot 1. Each year, lime is given to the plot which is to grow the brassica crop.

3
Physical Help

Most people starting on a new garden, or a newly-acquired garden, will grab a spade to make their first move. Instinctively, they feel that the quickest way to tidy the ground is to hide all the weeds and debris by digging it in. When you have made your assessment, as suggested in the previous chapter, you too will have that urge to grab a spade and get on with it – with perhaps just a touch of restraint. Indeed, there is no doubt that digging of some sort should have a high priority.

First, if you are taking on a garden during the growing season, you should knock down any tall weed growth, using a sickle or a billhook, and stack it in a corner to be composted or left to rot down. The object of this is not just to make the place look tidy, but also to check weeds by reducing the risk of seeding and by interrupting root-growth. Assuming, for the moment, that there is no drainage problem (this will be dealt with later in this chapter), you can simply carry on with clearing and digging, so as to get rid of unwanted plants and objects, and let air into the soil.

BURIED TOPSOIL

When making a garden on what we call 'virgin soil' or unbroken ground, you should first mark off pathways and places you will not be planting. The remainder should then be cleared of debris and surface growth ready for digging. If it is the garden of a newly-built house there may be some bits of building material that you can use for path-making, but there may also be some patches where the surface has been levelled off with clay subsoil dug from the foundations. In the latter case, with careful spade-work you may be able to restore some of the good surface soil to its rightful position.

I tried to dig out buried topsoil for just this reason some years ago, in the back garden of a newly-built house. My next-door neighbour, with several weeks' start on me, had learned that our plots had formerly been a hollow. The builder had spread clay, dug from the foundations of several houses, to level it off. This neighbour had the bright idea of putting the dumped clay to one side, digging out the buried topsoil, then putting in the clay and spreading the topsoil on the surface. When I tried this, I found that my plot covered the deeper end of the hollow and sloped steeply down. At times I had to move more than three feet of clay to reach the old surface of topsoil. It was a long and arduous job – but the worst was to come. This excavating left the subsoil lumpy and airy, and I spread the topsoil without allowing enough time for the ground to settle. Within a few weeks, all my lovely, light topsoil had washed down and disappeared.

The lesson to be learned here is that where subsoil is too free-draining, whether by nature or as the result of excavating, whatever is spread on the surface is liable to wash down or to have all soluble goodness leached out of it. Apart from the obvious need to allow ample time for ground to settle after digging, the remedy for this leaching problem is to put down ample fibre (such as peat) as a cushion *before* spreading light soil, or plant foods. In my case, the soil should have been given some months to settle after such unusually deep digging.

DOUBLE-DIGGING

One other problem some people come across with new gardens, is that the topsoil has been skimmed off and sold. On ground that neither drains too rapidly nor stands waterlogged, you may be able to restore surface tilth and fertility in a reasonable time by careful cultivation and feeding. Cultivating involves digging, forking and hoeing. Feeding is dealt with in Chapter 4, on nutrition.

The main aim of digging is to break up the soil and let it breathe, since air is an essential element. Normally the spade is thrust in to the full depth of its blade, 10in(25cm), and the spade full of soil is inverted as it is flung off. There is an old school of

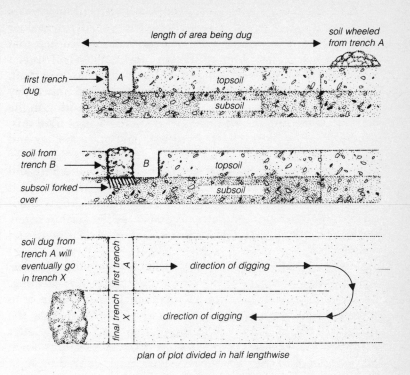

Fig 12   Double-digging.

thought which still maintains that double-digging is essential at times, and especially in breaking new ground. I have always suspected that double-digging and trenching (treble-digging) were invented by head gardeners just to keep all their men busy in winter, rather than for any good it did the soil. In those days, on big estates there was more than enough work to do most of the year – for instance, there was a great deal of bedding out (formal seasonal planting). Besides, when the master and mistress were entertaining a houseful of guests, there had to be extra supplies (fresh daily) of fruit, vegetables and flowers. The lawns had to be perfect and the flower-beds full of colour.

A big staff of gardeners was needed for all this work, but in quieter times the master was liable to observe that some of the men were not fully occupied. He would then cut down, and the remaining team of gardeners would be unable to cope adequately when busy times came round again. To avoid this loss of staff, head gardeners tried various ideas for keeping the men busy in winter. Double-digging was one such idea and if that was not enough to absorb all the labour, they tried treble-digging. I have done both, and am not satisfied that it brought enough soil improvement to justify the extra hard work. Perhaps that lack of satisfaction has made me too sceptical, but while double-digging may sometimes be helpful, I certainly do not advocate trenching.

Perhaps on ground that has not been dug or ploughed for some years, if it is heavy soil, and if you are keen to produce some prize vegetable for instance, you might find it worth while to double-dig. Double-digging does not mean digging the ground twice, but rather digging two spits deep – which will be to a depth of about 20in(50cm), a spit being the length of the blade of the spade, or about 10in(25cm) – in such a way as to keep the top spit on top.

Begin by digging a trench 1ft(30cm) wide and 1 spit deep, across the patch at one end; wheel the dug-up soil to the other end of the patch (*see* Fig 12). Now with fork or spade, turn over the soil in the bottom of the trench (this is the subsoil), breaking up lumps but leaving this subsoil where it was. At this stage, it helps to put a dressing of stable manure into the the trench. The manure can either be forked into the subsoil or left as a sponge to sit between topsoil and subsoil – this will depend on how heavy or light your soil is, and on what depth of root you are catering for.

Now dig the second 1ft(30cm) width of the surface, throwing this topsoil forward into the first trench. Where the ground is covered with grass growth, some gardeners skim this off, put it upside-down in the trench and chop it up before doing the rest of the filling-in. Whichever way you do it, you now find yourself with the second trench ready to be treated the same way as the first. Continue this pattern of digging until you reach the end of the patch, where the final trench can be filled by using the soil removed when digging the first.

Many people contend that the trench should be made 2ft(60cm) wide, to give more space for wielding the spade. That is the way I was taught to do it, and you can try that way if you prefer (the process being the same except for the measurements) – it does give more comfortable access to the trench, for turning the subsoil. I opted for 1ft(30cm) working to halve the quantity of soil that has to be carried away when digging that first trench. When you have a large patch to dig, you will find it worth while to divide it lengthways into two strips. You can then reduce the soil-wheeling if you work in one direction on the first strip and back in the opposite direction on the second strip. The soil dug from the first trench (on strip one) will not have to be moved far, as it can be used to fill the final trench on strip two (*see* Fig 12).

DIGGING-IN

The chief physical additive for soil improvement is undoubtedly humus-forming material, such as peat or leaf-mould, which should be thoroughly mixed into the soil with a spade or garden fork. It can open heavy, clay soil by mixing in amongst its fine particles which otherwise cling in a large mass and exclude air; while on sandy soil it can provide an element of sponginess to reduce the rapidity of the drying out process.

Clay soils can also be improved physically by adding coarse sand or grit, which is thoroughly dug in as prescribed for peat. Gypsum (calcium sulphate) physically helps clay by mixing the clay's minute particles and transforming them into grains, though only tiny ones. It can be used at a rate of 8oz(225g) to 1 square yard (0.8m^2) on stubborn clay. Lime has a similar effect, but to a smaller degree. Hydrated lime is best for clay soils and can be used at up to 1lb(450g) to 1 square yard (0.8m^2) – more on lime (including carbonate of lime for sandy soils) can be found in the next chapter.

Care should be taken when digging a shallow topsoil on solid clay, as annual inversion of the full top spit will slow down the process of soil improvement. For instance, if your top spit has only 3–4in(8–10cm) of friable (crumbly) soil, try not to bury it by inverting the full 10in(20cm) spit, and bringing stiff clay to the top. My experience is that the best way to cope with that sort of situation is to invert just the top 4–5in(10–12cm) at first, and subsequently to invert only 1in(2.5cm) more each year.

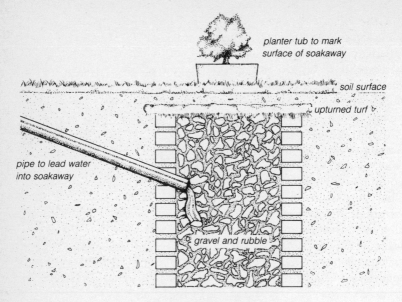

Fig 13   *The soakaway.*

THE SOAKAWAY

Where drainage is a problem, you may well be able to solve it by digging a soakaway or sump-hole, with drainage channels feeding into it. If you have done the test suggested in Chapter 2 – digging a hole about 2ft(60cm) deep and watching how quickly it drained – you will have decided whether or not you need to make a sump-hole.

However slight the slope, your soakaway should be sited at its lower end, to help surface water drain naturally. It should be at least 4ft(127cm) deep – ideally 6ft(180cm) – and must certainly be deep enough to go below any impervious layer. Before any drainage material is put into it, the hole should be left for a while, preferably during wet weather, so that you can check to see that it clears reasonably. The surface area of the hole depends on how deep you need to dig – it will have to be at least 2x2ft(50x50cm), but you may want to make it bigger to give yourself room to work, depending on the depth.

When in operation, it should cope with surface water, but deeper waterlogging calls for a channel, or channels, feeding into the hole and filled with stones and hard rubble. The channels should have a fall of about 1 in 20, towards the soakaway. My own formula is to fill the soakaway with good hard rubble to within 1ft(30cm) of the surface, then add some smaller rubble and finally a few upturned turves. I have also found it best always to have the hole marked clearly to remind me not to disturb it – a planted tub serves that need quite well.

In the average garden, it is unlikely that there will be a drainage problem that cannot be solved by an efficient soak-away, as described here. If the problem is too big for that, you would be best advised to consult your local drainage contractor. What you would need is a system such as a herring-bone pattern of trenches, with pipes and rubble. In an extensive area, such as farmland, there would be no problem in siting such a drainage system, but in the average garden you would still need soakaways or you would be liable merely to create problems for neighbours by channelling the drain water into their gardens. My advice, then, is to rely on soakaways or consult a specialist.

4
Soil Nutrition

Soil nutrition is the study of plant foods in the soil. This involves a great deal more than simply applying the right mixture of the three main mineral elements – nitrogen, phosphorus and potassium (commonly referred to by their chemical symbols, N, P, and K). These three are critical to plant health – nitrogen is necessary for leaf and shoot growth, phosphorus for root growth and potassium for flowers and fruit, although that is very much an over-simplification of a complicated process.

Calcium, magnesium and sulphur are also needed in varying amounts, and there are several other minerals, the so-called trace elements, which are needed in very small quantities. These trace elements include boron, chlorine, copper, iron, manganese, molybdenum and zinc. Scientists have diagnosed poor growth and sickness in specific plants as being due to a need for certain other elements. Some lime-haters require small quantities of aluminium, and some plants, such as legumes, need cobalt to help in the fixing and storing of nitrogen in root nodules. There is also evidence that some plants have benefited from the presence in the soil of small quantities of what are termed 'non-essentials' which seem to act like tonics or appetisers – cobalt, nickel, selenium, sodium, strontium and vanadium fall into this category. Bear these in mind next time you sprinkle a few grains of an NPK fertiliser on the soil around a hungry plant in the belief that you are giving it every kindness.

Furthermore, nutrition is not just a matter of lacing the soil with the right elements in carefully balanced proportions. The soil must be able to hold those elements in solution (plant roots absorb only liquids), which is where the physical improvements, discussed in the previous chapter, are important. And all these factors are influenced by day-length, temperature, moisture and all the bacteria and other life in the soil.

But don't be discouraged. You *can* improve your garden soil and your plants' performance in it simply by giving it NPK plant foods in the right quantities at the right time, without worrying yourself too much about all those other mineral elements, provided you have dealt with the physical factors outlined in the previous chapter. Nitrogen, phosphorus and potash, helped sometimes by calcium (lime), are the four chief chemicals you will need to apply to your garden soil, whatever may be needed by farmland and other commercial holdings.

LIQUID FERTILISERS

Supposing you were in charge of a large party of people going abroad on a holiday tour – you would pack what you thought was needed, including perhaps a few pills in case someone in the party had a stomach upset, due to change of climate, or indigestion due to unfamiliar foods. You would not be astounded if you had to shop during the holiday for other items you had not packed.

Similarly, when you are in charge of a large number of plants in a garden, and 99 subjects in every hundred flourish in your soil on your programme of plant feeding, you don't change the programme to suit the odd one. You might worry if you were a farmer growing that plant by the acre, or a commercial grower specialising in one subject (chrysanthemums, for example), when you could feel that you *must* find an answer. But as a gardener you could try a simpler remedy, such as re-siting the plant or varying its treatment, before worrying about the soil.

As gardeners, it is pleasing for us to know that we can vastly improve our soil by good cultivation and by enriching it with N, P, K and Ca (lime). But simply scattering granular or powdered fertiliser is not enough. We have to rely on it being washed in, then held by fibres in the soil, and in due time released gradually, in solution, to be taken up by plant roots. Liquid fertilisers get a quicker start than do solids, but just like the granules and powders they need to be picked up by fibres.

The proportion not picked up will be wasted by leaching away into underground streams.

The days when we had none of these chemical fertilisers are still well remembered by many of today's gardeners – for as long as anyone can remember, gardeners have tried to put back into the soil as much as they took out. They learned, from the failures of primitive cultivations, that the soil became exhausted by continual cropping and that in consequence crop yields got smaller and poorer. Not everyone could understand scientific talk about the 'nitrogen cycle' and the 'indestructibility of matter', but they did realise that when animal and vegetable waste was dug into the soil there was a great improvement in the quality and size of what was grown in it.

MANURING THE SOIL

The word manure stems from 'manoeuvre', which is from the French word meaning (among other things) to employ artifice and to manipulate by scheming or adroitness. So it seems that some artifice was accepted in the old methods of soil enrichment before manufactured fertilisers were disapprovingly dubbed 'artificials'.

All animal and vegetable waste was approved by our gardening forebears as helpful to the soil, and they dug in every kind of waste matter they could get their garden forks into. The gardeners' favourite was stable manure, which they called horse muck, and some people would even rush into the lane with a bucket and shovel to collect any left by passing horses – which were the main motive power for transport. Second favourite was farmyard manure, and with both these it was fully appreciated that their value to the soil was enhanced by the straw mixed with them.

Perhaps it was by accident of circumstance that we discovered the benefit of leaving manures to ferment in heaps (a form of composting), but well-rotted manures are more readily accepted by the soil during the growing season, fresh manure having a caustic and scorching effect if it comes into contact with tender roots or stems. The manure heap became an important feature of every garden. At first such heaps were left

36

exposed to the weather, but later it was realised that protection from rain was better. The general practice was to incorporate plenty of strawy manure during the autumn digging of vacant ground. It was also used as a thick mulch, applied to the surface soil around trees, shrubs and rose bushes. Those practices continue to be popular, especially among keen rosarians, wherever these bulk manures are still available.

Using Other Wastes

In addition to these types of manures, all available animal and vegetable wastes were used for soil improvement. The list included brewers' grains, spent hops, butchers' waste, discarded fish, fish guano, blood, bones, hair, leather waste and dust, hoof and horn, night soil, garden refuse, kitchen waste, green manure, poultry droppings, shoddy, and soot. Many of these items still find their way into the soil by various means, those which offend the eye or the nostrils being processed or treated to make them more acceptable.

If you tried using fish discards nowadays you would probably be contravening health regulations – in any event, such a practice would not be socially acceptable to the neighbours. But fish waste and discards are processed to make animal food as well as a fertiliser – the bones are treated against the risk of anthrax and sold mostly as bone-meal. Dried blood is also a popular fertiliser, and my own formula is to stir in hydrated lime – 1lb(0.45kg) to every 1 gallon (4.5 litres) – and leave the mixture to dry on a shallow tray. When dry, it crumbles into a powder that is rich in nitrogen (about 12 per cent) and clean to handle. Several of the other items on the list are no longer available in the raw form. You can get spent hops if you live near a brewery, but you would do better to buy hop manure, which is an enriched product manufactured from the hops.

Leather dust was used at one time, in the same way as sand, to add bulk to concentrated fertilisers and make accurate distribution easier. Alone, it is not valuable, as it offers only a very small amount of nitrogen, which is released slowly. Soot was popular with all gardeners in the days when the prevalence of coal fires made it readily available. It has a high nitrogen content as you can quickly prove by rubbing equal quantities of lime and soot together in the palms of the hands. The effect is to release ammonia, which has an unmistakable, strong smell.

This chemical reaction is the reason why lime and nitrogen-ous chemicals should not normally be mixed. The exception is where it is dug into the soil immediately on mixing, as a soil fumigant. In its fresh state, soot is caustic and should not be allowed to touch plants or their roots, but if put on the surface to encircle plants (clear of their leaves and stems) it will keep off slugs and flies. Before use as a plant nutrient, it should be stored in the open – sheltered from rain – for about four months to get rid of its caustic fumes. A bag of soot suspended in a rain barrel for a week or so will make a liquid manure the colour of weak tea, which is just about right for plant feeding.

It is interesting to look more closely at some of the items mentioned. Stable manure and farmyard manures have much the same qualities. Stable manure is usually lighter physically and is better, especially with long straw, for use on heavy, clay soils. Cow and pig manures, preferably with shorter (partly chopped) straw, are better for sandy soils. Both have a high straw content – unless someone has been too mean with the animals' bedding – and the straw has usually become saturated with urine which helps to break it down.

What is supplied under the general description of farmyard manure will usually be mainly from cattle. Sometimes it

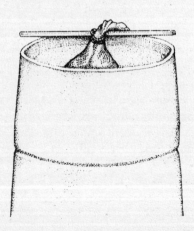

Fig 14   Bag of soot in water barrel.

includes stable manure and more rarely some from pig-pens. The pig manure is usually kept separate and of course there are pig farms, where no other animals are kept. When it is fresh, pig manure has a smell that offends most people, and which tends to linger. For gardening purposes, therefore, it is better avoided until it has completed its fermentation. Also see that it contains enough straw.

Where There's Muck . . .

There was a saying in Lancashire and Yorkshire at the height of the Industrial Revolution: ' Where there's muck, there's brass'. 'Brass' meant money, and the implication was that the grime of the mills was worth putting up with because it was an inescapable by-product of the profitable manufacture of cotton, linen, and other goods.

In another context, concerning the incorporation of farm and stable muck into the soil, it might equally be said that 'Where there's muck, there's rich soil'. Our ancestors knew it but were not sure why. They greatly overestimated the nutrient content of farmyard and stable manures, which is much less than most people still imagine. The secret of the nourishing effects these manures have in the soil lies first in their loose bulk (which helps control the vital air and moisture) and then in their humus-making capacity. They absorb and transform complex substances in the soil, and later release them in assimilable form as plant nutrients which the roots are able to take up. This explains why they are a powerful aid to soil nutrition even though their basic nutrient content is not high.

Manures vary tremendously from farm to farm, and their maximum nutrient content is 1.3 per cent nitrogen, 0.5 per cent phosphorus, and 0.25 per cent potassium. For comparison, the National Growmore formula (devised as an all-purpose general fertiliser during World War II) yields 7 per cent nitrogen, 7 per cent phosphorus and 7 per cent potassium. Perhaps that explains why, in the days before chemical fertilisers, farmers and gardeners alike felt it necessary to use bulk manures in such large quantities when in a hurry to get high yields from their crops. You can reckon that 1 ton (1.016 tonnes) of farm manure equals only 20lb(9kg) of nitrogen, but remember its other qualities, especially in the long term.

PROCESSED FERTILISERS

Farm and stable manures are now being dried and processed commercially, and sold off the shelf alongside other garden fertilisers, against which they can compete successfully. They are pleasant to handle and rich in plant nutrients. These of course do not have the humus-making bulk of the raw product, which you may find impossible to get anyway, unless you live near a source of supply.

Fish waste is much richer than farmyard manures (although its nutrient content is also variable), yielding up to a possible maximum of 10 per cent nitrogen and 14 per cent phosphorus, plus just a little potassium. The raw material has been replaced, for gardening purposes, by a processed fish manure which has no unpleasant smell and which gives up to 10 per cent nitrogen, 12 per cent phosphorus and 1 per cent potassium. Fish guano is a similar fertiliser, processed from the waste collected from factories smoking and canning fish. It yields up to 10 per cent nitrogen, 9 per cent phosphorus and 3 per cent potassium.

In the days before the present strict regulations controlling animal slaughter, the butcher's midden was a source of animal waste for some gardeners. The waste was collected and dug in promptly, because delay meant that blowflies would be attracted and the stuff would soon be crawling with maggots. All such material nowadays is hygienically dealt with at the abattoirs and sent for processing.

Blood is a rich source of nitrogen and it too was collected, poured into shallow drills and dug in promptly. It was also mixed with lime, as previously described, and dried to make a powder. The commercial product, powdered dried blood, contains about 12 per cent nitrogen. It is applied, at 2oz(50g) to 1 square yard (0.83 m^2), to the soil around plants in full growth, and is sometimes brought back to liquid form – 1oz(25g) to 1 gallon (4.5 litres) of water – before use. Dried blood is used also in some potting composts.

Shoddy (wool and silk waste), and hair (mainly the scraping from hides at the tanneries), were in more plentiful supply before man-made fibres came into cloth production and plastics displaced some leather. They have a variable but substantial nitrogen content (5–15 per cent) and are good slow-release fertilisers. They are valuable also as bulky manures, especially the shoddy which comes from wool.

It is interesting to reflect on what we get from the sheep apart from the meat, as we seem to find a use for every scrap of the animal. Its wool yields lanolin, the basis of so many beauty treatments and ointments, before being spun and woven for cloth. The waste from the mills gives us shoddy, which now goes mostly for processing, as does the hair. Hoof and horn, as you may guess, comes from the feet and heads of cattle and sheep, and the hooves of horses, and is similar to hard bones but cleaner. This is still available as a fertiliser, yielding 12–14 per cent nitrogen. Even though broken into tiny bits, it dissolves very slowly in the soil and does an excellent job in keeping pot soil viable after other fertilisers have been consumed or washed out. The rate of use in potting composts is only 1½oz(35g) to the bushel (36.4 litres). Outdoors it is applied at 2oz(50g) to 1 square yard (0.8m²).

Night Soil

Night soil was an important manure for farming up to the early 1900s, and to a lesser extent for gardening. Weight for weight it is far richer than farmyard or stable manures. Before modern sanitations, earth closets were in general use and many of these led into middens into which was thrown all kitchen and household refuse – and a fair amount of disinfectant. In some areas, the household refuse included large quantities of coal ash, especially in places within easy reach of pit-heads, where low transport costs made coal a cheap fuel. Coal was needed not just to heat the home, but also to stoke the oven for cooking, and to heat water for all domestic purposes including the family wash. Farmers on heavy clay did not mind the ash, though it was not so useful on sandy soils.

The name night soil probably stems from the normal practice in most areas of collecting this refuse at night, partly because conditions were cooler in those hours and no doubt partly for social reasons. On farms, night soil was spread immediately on arrival and left unploughed until a whole field had been treated. For gardens, some night soil was collected privately and discreetly and dug in promptly. Its soil improvement potential was much cherished by keen gardeners aiming to win prizes at shows. Modern sanitation saw earth closets disappear from all but remote places, to be replaced by water closets, but it took many years before main sewage pipes were extended to all areas. Meanwhile, cesspits were dug in country areas and tankers known affectionately as 'lavender carts' or 'honey wagons' pumped them out at regular intervals. The loads from these tankers were then spread on farmland – a practice which was still in use in some remote areas until recently.

To avoid total loss of this source of soil nutrition, sewage disposal experts made scientific experiments aimed at processing the sludge into a powdered fertiliser, odourless and easy to handle. Sewage sludge does not have a high nutrient content – it has little more than two per cent nitrogen and rather less of phosphorus. When dried, poultry droppings are richer than farmyard manure, containing about four per cent nitrogen, three per cent phosphorus and over one per cent potassium. Its bulk will vary with the amount and type of litter used for the poultry.

Garden refuse can be dug straight into the soil but it is much better when properly composted (as will be described later).

Green Manuring

Green manuring is the practice of growing a quick-maturing crop, such as mustard, to dig straight into the ground just before it goes to seed, which is a useful way of helping sandy and similar soils which are short of humus. The disadvantage of this practice, and that of digging-in garden refuse uncomposted, is that although the ultimate result is to add nitrogen to the soil, the immediate effect is to take some away. This is because the vegetable matter absorbs nitrogen to help it decompose. To overcome this when green manuring, farmers sometimes dress the green manure crop with a nitrogenous fertiliser, such as sulphate of ammonia or nitro chalk immediately before turning it in. Besides correcting the temporary loss of nitrogen, this dressing also helps the crop to rot down more quickly – but it is not essential, unless the aim is to save time. Wherever any of the manures in the foregoing list is used regularly, there will probably be a need for a dressing of lime to neutralise acidity or souring of the soil. This should not be done haphazardly, but on the basis of a careful analysis of the soil's requirements. The procedure for such tests ties up with that used for assessing fertiliser needs (*see* page 18).

NUTRIENT CONTENTS

A fertiliser is anything which helps to make soil fertile or productive, but in farming and gardening practice the term is restricted to those fertilisers which do not come under the heading of manure and, more strictly, only to those which contain, in concentrated form, one or more of the three major elements – nitrogen, phosphorus, and potassium. Manufacturers are obliged by law to state the proportions of these three elements on the package. If you find a bag marked 'NPK fertiliser 15–15–21', it means that the fertiliser provides the three main elements in the ratio of 15N, 15P and 21K, N being the symbol for nitrogen, P for phosphorus and K for potassium. The marking will probably indicate what proportion of the phosphates are quick acting (soluble), the remainder being slow to dissolve. It will also specify what minor elements (if any) are included in the mixture – for example, Mg indicates magnesium.

Concentrated fertilisers, rather than manures, are the most-used form of soil nutrition these days. They are sometimes condemned as chemicals in the mistaken belief that all chemicals are inorganic and bad. In fact the main plant elements can be obtained as organic fertilisers. The practice of organic gardening is a much wider subject and is discussed later in this chapter.

The three main elements in plant nutrition (N, P, K) are consumed in varying degrees by plants. Hence the soil must be suitably enriched by them in the first place to enable it to support plant life, and must be further enriched at intervals to restore what the plants take out.

In the earliest days of the move over from farmyard manures to concentrates, gardeners dabbled a great deal in making their own NPK mixtures. The chief source of nitrogen was sulphate of ammonia (others being nitrate of soda and dried blood). The phosphorus element was supplied by superphosphate of lime which despite its name, makes no significant contribution to the lime content. The potassium element was sulphate of potash or muriate of potash. Other items used occasionally in these home mixes included dried blood (for its nitrogen), bone-meal (chiefly for its phosphorus), and magnesium sulphate, which is also known as epsom salts (for its magnesium).

For brassicas, while accepting that leaves need the nitrogen, the best balance was deemed to be:

2 parts (by weight) sulphate of ammonia
3 parts superphosphate of lime
1 part sulphate of potash
Application rate: 3oz(75g) to 1 square yard (0.8m^2)

For root crops, other than potatoes, the emphasis was on phosphorus and the accepted mixture was:

1 part sulphate of ammonia
4 parts superphosphate of lime
2 parts sulphate of potash
Application rate: 4oz(100g) to 1 square yard (0.8m^2)

Potatoes need more potassium than other root crops, and for early varieties the mixture was:

5 parts sulphate of ammonia
8 parts superphosphate of lime
3 parts sulphate of potash
Application rate: 4oz(100g) to 1 square yard (0.8m^2)

For maincrop (late) varieties the emphasis changed to:

3 parts sulphate of ammonia
4 parts superphosphate of lime

2 parts sulphate of ammonia
Application rate: 5oz(125g) to 1 square yard (0.8m^2)

Fruit trees, as previously mentioned, require some emphasis on potassium but do not need much phosphorus – this element was usually provided in alternate years, in the shape of a dressing of basic slag, at the rate of 4oz(100g) to 1 square yard (0.8m^2) in October. The basic annual mixture was:

2 parts sulphate of ammonia
1 part sulphate of potash
Application rate: 3oz(75g) to 1 square yard (0.8m^2), in February–March

All these do-it-yourself mixtures may be deemed to be soundly based, though perhaps not so sophisticated as the commercial mixtures now more generally used. The straight fertilisers – as the components of these mixes are known when considered alone – are still sold, but are not so readily available as the proprietary fertiliser mixtures which are sold off the shelf.

ORGANIC GARDENING

One weakness of dry chemical feeding is that it cannot alone ensure sustained soil fertility. The process of nitrification is important to plant nutrition and depends on micro-organisms which thrive in the humus-forming organic matter.

This organic matter is provided by the remains of plant and animal materials which either arrive in the soil naturally, or are applied by the gardener. They come naturally as plants die, leaves fall, and so on, or are applied in various forms, such as farmyard manures, garden composts, and peat. We recognise them chiefly as fibrous material, which is capable of holding moisture and those essential micro-organisms.

When the shortage of organic matter becomes acute, the soil is reduced to dust, which can be picked up by the wind and carried off, thus quickly and severely eroding its fertility. In large-scale cereal farming, this soil erosion can bring chaos almost overnight during dry or windy weather, after the harvesting of a crop has exposed the soil surface. Rebuilding the soil's fertility by the addition of adequate bulky material can take some years. Everyone, therefore, recognises the vital need for organic matter in the maintenance of soil quality, and no good gardener ignores it. Manufactured chemical fertilisers are used by most gardeners only as crop boosters, while garden compost, peat and other bulky materials are added as the basis of soil fertility. But there is a large section of the farming and gardening public which goes further and declares that these chemicals should not be used at all. These are the people who favour what is called organic gardening, though not all give the same definition of the term. It is a bit like defining vegetarianism, in that some apply the principles more strictly than do others. There are some gardeners who practise organic gardening in the matter of soil nutrition only, but the true converts have a back-to-nature approach to all problems of pest and disease control.

This second aspect is the difficult one in practice. On diseases, the theory is that a soil enriched only by animal and other organic manures will be healthy and that a healthy soil will resist disease organisms. On pests, the belief is that if nature is left alone she will help to find a proper balance. But nature can be cruel – swarms of locusts regularly devour whole crops in some parts of Africa. If we dispense with modern aids to pest and disease control we need to do a great deal of extra work keeping the troubles in check. Some claim that marigold grown among tomatoes will keep out whitefly; others say it is not so. Some claim that nasturtiums will keep off greenfly, but others say they avoid nasturtiums because the undersides of the leaves are always smothered in blackfly, which are as bad as greenfly. All these claims are truthful but are based on experiences and circumstances that differ widely.

The way to decide convincingly would be to commit the whole garden to exclusively organic treatment. You could experiment with organic fertilisers on part of the garden, while using whatever other methods you like on the rest. By comparing the results, you could then decide which method best suited your needs. But the same practice would not do for comparing methods of pest and disease control, because there is no reasonable means of making the troubles respect the artificial boundaries of your experimental plots. Indeed, even when using your whole garden as the experimental areas, you cannot ensure that no trouble will reach it from neighbouring gardens. Therefore, if you want to commit yourself to organic gardening you must take a gamble.

ORGANIC FERTILISERS

Every garden ought to have a compost heap, and the organic gardener relies heavily on compost as a soil conditioner and source of plant nutrients. All vegetable waste goes on to the compost heap. Details on composting are given later – but there are other soil additives which may be used in organic gardening, and which you can of course try out on marked areas of your soil first.

There are several proprietary brands of general fertilisers which are made by processing manures from farms and stables – you will find them in shops and garden centres. A typical example, one that I use regularly, is called Stimgro, which is made from cow manure and peat; Cowpact and Farmura are other similar products.

Bone-meal is commonly available and is used as a slow-acting source of phosphorus on strawberries, roses and other plants. Rock potash is favoured as a source of potash for potatoes, beans and tomatoes. Seaweed is the base of several general fertilisers, including liquids such as Maxicrop. Dolomite contains magnesium carbonate as well as lime, and is used instead of lime where there is a magnesium deficiency. Gypsum (magnesium sulphate) is accepted by all gardeners as an aid to breaking up heavy clay. It can also be mixed with Dolomite for the same purpose. Worms are great allies of the gardener and their casts are now sold as a fertiliser. Those old natural products, blood, fish, bones, hooves and horns are all offered in various forms as general fertilisers.

While relying on nature to maintain a healthier environment than is generally found in gardens where manufactured chemicals are used, most organic gardeners accept some pesticides as harmless to friendly creatures. These are available from sources catering for such gardeners. Quassia chips and soft soap, for example, have been mixed for generations to make a liquid spray against caterpillars and other small pests. Nicotine, derris and pyrethrum are three more old favourite insecticides. Fertosan is an excellent natural slug-killer, and copper sulphate remains popular as a fungicide, in Bordeaux mixture.

No matter how far you choose to go, it will be clear that you cannot transform a garden from orthodox to organic in one season, so whatever experiments you make will need to be continued for some years, and you must be prepared for disappointments. Before you embark on organic gardening on a large scale, you should spend some time studying the subject. You will find for instance that its practitioners prefer seed that has been organically grown rather than any produced by orthodox methods. Advice on what to read is available from The Soil Association (*see* Useful Addresses).

5
The Compost Heap

As horse transport was phased out to be replaced by cars, lorries, vans, buses and tramcars, gardeners had problems finding stable manure. When tractors took over from horses on the farm, it was not surprising that farmers kept most of their farmyard manure for their own fields. Soon, the compost heap became recognised as a vital alternative source of supply of fibrous material. The earliest edition of the Royal Horticultural Society's *Dictionary of Gardening*, published in 1951, included the following short entry under the heading, 'Compost-Heap':

'The conversion of vegetable refuse into manure has become essential now that farmyard and stable manure is so much less abundant, for the maintenance of a high humus content in our soils is a necessity for high fertility for most of the plants we grow.'

Another entry on the same page indicates that up to that time a different meaning had always been attributed to the word compost, and still is. It illustrates why the word causes confusion in some people's minds. Compost can mean on the one hand a mixture for seed sowing or potting, and on the other hand a manure made from vegetable and other refuse. Interestingly enough, this second entry in the dictionary is clearly concerned with the larger gardens cultivated by most Fellows of the Royal Horticultural Society at that time – nowadays the society's membership is bigger and more comprehensive. Under the heading 'Compost-Yard', it defines such a yard as:

'An enclosure in a garden, preferably near the potting sheds, where different soils, manures, etc. are stored until required. Part of the area should be under cover, as an open shed, where composts can be made in wet weather and kept dry for use. This shed should have a concrete floor. Each material in the yard should have its proper place and the whole area should be kept tidy.'

The compost referred to in this paragraph is obviously the loam, sand, peat, leaf-mould, manure and other material used to make potting and sowing mixtures. Usually you can rely on the context to make clear in which sense the word is being used, but take care to avoid confusion. For my part, I usually refer to the product of the waste heap as garden compost.

In the first entry quoted, the dictionary sums up excellently and briefly the reason why our soil needs garden compost these days. However, it does not claim to deal with any method of the 'conversion of vegetable refuse into manure' to which it refers. And that is not so easy.

If you go into any town or suburban garden and look for the compost heap, too often all you will find is a corner where weed, exhausted plants, and the unwanted parts of vegetables have been dumped casually. This should not be called a compost heap. Sometimes you will see that a serious attempt has been made to build a tidy heap. But a little prodding into the heap with a garden fork will reveal only some soggy rubbish that is more likely to putrify into a smelly, wet mass than to turn into the crumbly, soil-like stuff with a pleasant, earthy smell that we call garden compost.

CONSTRUCTING COMPOST HEAPS

To begin with, you need to think of two heaps, rather than one, because after a heap is completed it needs months – varying according to the season – to complete the fermentation. Indeed keen composters may have three heaps: one fully converted and ready for use; one complete but still working; and the third in process of building. Even so there may have to be a further small, temporary stack of material (perhaps lawn mowings) which has to be held back until the right volume of other waste is available to mix with it.

The heap can be built on bare soil, giving the worm population access to help with the work. It is not essential to have any sort of structure to contain the heap, though most people prefer it for the sake of tidiness. You will find a well-sharpened spade useful, first for chopping up refuse before putting it on the heap, and next (unless the heap is boxed in), for trimming the sides at times as the stuff settles down. The area of the heap or structure should be about 4x4ft(120x120cm), and the ultimate height about the same or not more than 5ft(150cm). Some people enclose all four sides, and some enclose three, to have access from the front. The sides can be of timber, brick or wire netting. If timber or bricks are used, it is essential that they are not made solid, as a good free flow of air is needed.

It is helpful to consider what materials are likely to be composted before making a decision on what type of structure or proprietary container to use. Enthusiasts say that anything from vegetable or animal sources will make compost. This is true in theory and, where time allows, it may prove quite correct, but some material is extremely slow to break down and it is not practical to treat all waste as of equal value for

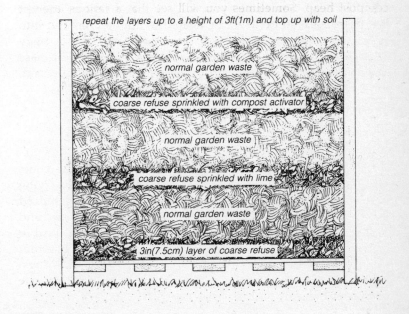

repeat the layers up to a height of 3ft(1m) and top up with soil

normal garden waste

coarse refuse sprinkled with compost activator

normal garden waste

coarse refuse sprinkled with lime

normal garden waste

3in(7.5cm) layer of coarse refuse

Fig 15   Building the compost heap.

composting. Old leather boots, for instance, would take much longer than cabbage leaves and would probably come out whole when the rest of the heap is fully composted.

More practically than old boots, you should think of woody prunings from roses, trees and shrubs. A small amount of this material – say a 3–4in(8–10cm) layer – will make a good base for the heap if followed by a 9in(23cm) layer of soft material. After that base layer, woody prunings even when chopped up thoroughly do not, in my experience, break down within the normal life of a heap. I prefer to burn them and be content to collect the wood ash as their contribution to soil fertility.

However, there are small, wood-chipping machines available for domestic use. Keen composters use these to grind down all woody material and put it on the compost heap. If you care to try that idea, I suggest you mix the chips well into plenty of soft waste. You may also need to use extra nitrogen to help break it down.

Keeping the Heap Healthy

Other material which should never be put on the compost heap is anything infected with soil-borne diseases. These diseases usually show themselves clearly enough to make the gardener

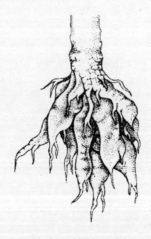

Fig 16   Brassica root infected by club root.

wary. But I have known people put infected young cabbage or Brussels sprout plants on the compost heap, thinking that they were safe because the infection had not gone far. The disease in that case was club root, which when fully developed in the roots and stem will make a huge swelling and a horrible smell. The first hint of this fungal disease is enough to bar the plant from the compost heap.

Some plants can live with club root long enough to make useful hearts for eating. This is achieved by treating the roots with a mercury preparation (calomel) from the seedling stage, so that the plant can make plenty of growth before the fungus gets into the tissues. On infected land, where the alternative is to abandon all brassica cultivation for seven or more years, such a practice is not unreasonable. But the smallest hint of club root condemns the plant as unfit for the compost heap – where it would multiply and infect the whole heap. All suspected brassicas, such as turnips, cabbages, sprouts and any such crops grown on suspected soil, however clean they may look, should go in the incinerator.

Another soil fungus trouble, rarely seen now thanks to regulations restricting the use of susceptible plants, is wart disease of potatoes. It is a notifiable disease, so if you suspect it among your potatoes you must report it. Again, you should have a garden incinerator and make sure you destroy infected material by fire. If you grow potatoes, you should learn to recognise common scab so as not to confuse it with warts, but when in doubt treat any potato as too suspect for the heap. Blight, which attacks potatoes and tomatoes, is another fungus to stamp out as quickly as possible by consigning infected material to the incinerator.

Most airborne diseases are usually destroyed by good composting. That is, the temperature generated in the heap should be high enough to take care of such matters. However, I am more concerned with controlling pests and diseases in my garden than with accumulating the maximum quantity of stuff for composting. If I have any suspicions, my rule is, 'when in doubt, find out'. But the safety-first policy is to put doubtful stuff straight into the incinerator and make sure a good fire burns it up right away. When you are not sure that you can find out in time, play for safety with all diseased and infected material, and burn it.

After you have used a hormone-type weed-killer on the lawn, the next three or four weeks' clippings are not safe to put on the compost heap or on the ground around cultivated plants.

Suitable Materials

Apart from the unsuitable items mentioned, almost any material of vegetable or animal origin may be composted, including uncooked waste from the kitchen (I prefer to avoid cooked food waste). But do take care to handle all such waste in a way that does not encourage vermin or marauding dogs. Keep it secure before it goes on the heap and have it adequately buried in the heap afterwards. When there is doubt, it is much better to put stuff on the incinerator than to risk encouraging vermin or foxes.

When building your compost heap you should keep in mind from the start that the clever little micro-organisms responsible for the decomposition of whatever material you put on it cannot work without an adequate supply of nitrogen. Some of this nitrogen they can get from the air, provided the heap is to their liking, but this will not be enough to ensure speedy decomposition. To hurry things on a bit, a large part of the nitrogen must be provided by additives such as nitrogenous fertilisers or manures – these are generally known as 'compost accelerators'.

Besides the nitrogen, from whatever source, the heap needs a flow of air into and through it. Moisture is also essential in about the same ratio as is needed in soil which is sustaining plant life, which means it must not dry out but must never be so wet as to squeeze out the air.

Controlling and Stacking

The main needs of your compost heap, then, are nitrogen, ventilation and moisture; your aim must be to control and stack the waste matter in such a way as to meet all three demands constantly. Control means having the waste in the best possible condition before putting it on the heap. Stacking involves mixing the different wastes so that they help each other, putting them on in successive layers and treating each layer in turn. Layers should be about 6–9in(15–23cm) thick, depending to some extent on the materials. For instance, if the waste is dry it should be trodden down well, but if it is green and full of moisture it should be stacked rather more loosely. Either way, nitrogen should be added immediately. This can take the form of animal manure – to make a layer of about 2in(5cm) – or a sprinkling of sulphate of ammonia or nitro-chalk at a handful to 1 square yard (0.8m^2). A proprietary additive can be used instead and should be applied as directed by the manufacturers.

When the second layer of waste is added, give it an immediate soaking, followed by a liberal dusting of lime. Don't put the lime on until after the soaking or it will wash down to the nitrogen fertiliser. This pattern can be continued until the heap is completed – you may then consider turning your heap, as described below. Some composters prefer to apply the nitrogen to two or three successive layers and use lime on every third or fourth. Composting is not an exact science and there are many variable factors besides seasons and weather, so be guided by your judgement. Packets of proprietary accelerators may carry printed directions concerning the addition of lime to the heap.

Those who practise organic gardening will not use sulphate of ammonia, nitro-chalk, or the normal run of proprietary accelerators. Instead they prefer to rely on animal manures to add to each layer of waste. Fanatics try to get as close as they can to the soil conditions existing before manufactured chemicals were introduced, to the days of primitive sanitation. They even resort to the use of the old chamber pots and a few other tricks, on the basis that urine is the best activator of all. For those who are keen on avoiding manufactured chemical additives there are substitutes available. Firms which cater specially for the organic gardener retail a compost activator made entirely from herbal ingredients.

The length of time a heap takes to decompose into compost ready for use in the soil is influenced by various factors. A guide is that a heap built in summer should produce compost inside six months, but a heap built later in the year is not likely to be ready to dig in less than eight months.

Turning the Heap

Some gardeners like to turn the heap as soon as it heats up – which takes only a matter of days, and may be before your second layer is put on. The elaborate way to turn the heap is to dig it out and re-stack it on an adjacent spot. In this movement the outsides of the heap are re-stacked in the middle. Another method is to fork it over where it lies, but again trying to bring the middle to the outside. Either procedure calls for spare time and muscle-power as well as enthusiasm. Some enthusiasts wait until the heap has been completed and has cooled down, and then turn it over by re-stacking it on the adjacent site, so leaving the first site ready for the start of another stack. Many people do not attempt any of this extra work of turning, especially those who use special 'compost bins'.

Containers

The sort of container you choose to use for composting your garden waste is not critical to the success or failure of the process, or the quality of the compost. The size, shape and layout of your garden are factors which will influence the siting of the heap. The more difficult it is to hide that site, the more care is needed to make it look tidy. Furthermore, it is not just one heap you will have to contend with, but a minimum of two, and quite likely four. The second heap is absolutely essential while you are waiting for the first completed heap to finish working. Two should be enough for what some people term 'the average garden' or for anything but an outsized garden. Exceptions are where imported material is being brought in or crops are being grown specifically to make large quantities of compost – such as is done by organic gardeners. In addition to the two or three heaps in the process of composting, I have always found it helpful to have a temporary heap, for material 'in waiting'. For example, when large quantities of grass clippings are being dumped twice weekly they should be held back until there is enough other material to go with them to ensure a good, balanced mixture.

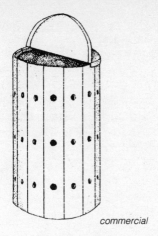

commercial

Fig 17(a)   Compost bins.

These thoughts highlight the point that screening would help improve the look of the garden. So when choosing your compost container think also of a bit of hedging or fencing to avoid having an eyesore.

Manufactured containers are readily available. Those seen most often are made of stout plastic and are barrel-shaped. A lid prevents leaching or cooling in wet weather. All these containers are designed to let in air at or near the bottom. Such containers, usually sold as 'compost bins', are ideal where only small quantities of waste are being composted. Filling them is no more difficult than dropping refuse into a rubbish bin, and they do not look unsightly.

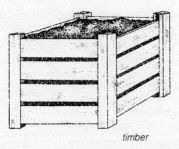

timber

Fig 17(b)

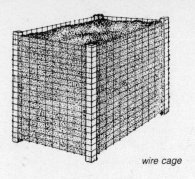

wire cage

Fig 17(c)

For larger quantities of waste, there are square-section bins available, perhaps 3x3ft(90x90cm) at the base. Those I have seen are collapsible, for easy transport from shop to garden, and will stand firm with one side removed for access while the heap is being built. Enthusiasts who wish to make large volumes of compost usually build their own structures, and the most popular base size is 4x4ft(120x120cm).

The easiest and cheapest to make is an open-topped cage of wire netting. For this, four corner-posts, 2x2in(5x5cm) or thicker are hammered into the ground, and the netting is wired or stapled around them. Such a container is not pretty and would normally be screened. A plastic netting, such as Netlon, is not an eyesore and has the more important advantage of being much longer lasting. I have a fence of Netlon which has been up for about 20 years and seems indestructible.

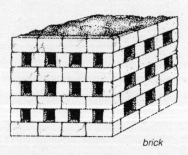

brick

Fig 17(d)

However, for a more permanent compost corner, a structure of brick or stout timber, or a combination of the two, will last a long time. If using timber, it is best to make the three sides separately and then set them up in position before bolting or screwing them together. Points to watch are that the feet (the bases of the uprights) are adequately soaked in preservative to prevent rotting, and that the open front is secure, and does not move when the loose boards used to close the gap are not in place. Sometimes suitable timber can be bought second-hand. It can be of whatever dimensions are readily obtainable but, ideally, should be 6in(15cm) wide and 1¼in(3cm) thick. Treat it in advance with a preservative such as Bio Woody, which is fungicidal and not caustic. Similar boards will be needed for the open side of a brick structure, and for upright battens to hold the boards in place.

The side boards of a timber structure should not be fitted closely but set up 1in(2.5cm) apart to let in air. The walls of a brick structure should have gaps near the bottom for the same purpose. Similarly, the front boards of any structure (brick or timber) should have about an inch gap between them. This can be achieved crudely by wedging them apart as you drop them in. Instead of loose boards, some gardeners prefer a full side, ventilated by a number of drilled holes, and resting on a couple of half-bricks.

Whatever system or structure you favour, remember to give cover against heavy rain when necessary as you build the heap. Remember also that when the heap is complete you must top it up with a layer of soil, well firmed, and again give it shelter from the weather.

6

Greenhouse, Frame and Parlour

SOIL IN THE GREENHOUSE

There are two distinct soil environments in greenhouses. One is that of earthy soil in the border, and the other is that of the subjects grown in pots. Both are somewhat sheltered or artificial – pot soil obviously so, and border soil rather less so.

Plants in pots or other indoor containers, in greenhouse or home, depend entirely on us to provide soil or other root medium, plus light, water, air and warmth.

The greenhouse border too is sheltered and cannot control its own supply of water, air, light and warmth, but it is in contact with the earth, from which it is able to draw a restricted supply of moisture, plus the benefit of some natural bacterial assistance. What we put into that border soil and what we take out of it will influence the length of its useful life, and it is not an uncommon practice among greenhouse gardeners, from time to time, to dig it out and replace it with soil dug from the open garden.

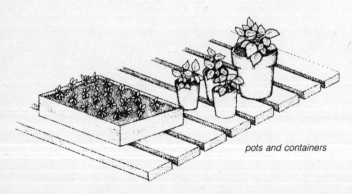

pots and containers

Fig 18(a)   Methods of growing.

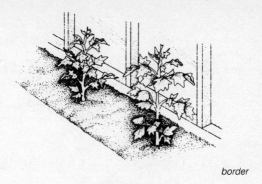

border

Fig 18(b)

Considering border soil first, what improvement it needs must obviously depend partly on its nature, and partly on what is to be grown in it, as is the case with soil in the open, but also on the intensity of the cropping. For instance, if you use the minimum of heat and take only seasonal crops of salad vegetables and tomatoes the soil needs only routine enrichment with fertilisers, control of water and ventilation, plus shading for the plants in extremely hot weather. The commercial grower of tomatoes, however, extending the season considerably and cropping his plants more heavily, will maintain a constant flow of extra nutriment. In fact nowadays he is more likely not to plant in the ground but to use bolster-like bags of rooting

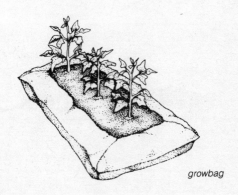

growbag

Fig 18(c)

medium, plus a sort of drip feed. There are commercial growers of other specialist crops – of which carnations, year-round chrysanthemums, roses, cucumbers and salad crops are just a few examples – whose methods with soil and other growing media do not apply to domestic greenhouse gardening.

Some soil problems met by commercial growers are due to monoculture, and these concern the domestic gardener too if he tries, as so many do, to grow his favourite crop year after year in the same soil. Of these problems, virus troubles are probably the worst, since they are almost impossible to eliminate, but there are others, which will be dealt with later. For the meantime we should note the point that, indoors as well as out, the soil can do better where the crop is varied yearly (crop rotation), and may even fail altogether with a crop of which it has grown 'sick'.

SOIL SICKNESS

Soil sickness is normally prevented outdoors by crop rotation – the system of organised switching of crop types, so that they get a change of soil each year. That system is not practical in a greenhouse, and the alternative is to change the soil or attempt to cleanse it of pests and diseases – a process which is termed sterilising but does not actually make the soil sterile. The aim of this so-called sterilising of soil is similar to that of milk pasteurising, that is, to treat it no further than is needed to kill the harmful elements in it.

The heat method is perhaps easiest to understand. Soil is heated to somewhere approaching, but not right up to, boiling point, in the hope of killing off insect pests, harmful bacteria, weed seeds and fungi without going so far as to make the soil inert. Steam heat is used commercially for this treatment, but it is not practical on a small scale.

Formaldehyde Treatment

Formaldehyde treatment is practical but laborious and unpleasant because the vapour given off can be irritating to the eyes and nose and has a strong smell. It works best in warm conditions and certainly should not be done in frosty weather. The method is to spread the soil on the concrete floor of the garage or other covered building, and water it with a solution made up of ¼ pint (140ml) of formaldehyde to 1½ gallons (6.75 litres) of water. Have the soil reasonably moist to start with and spread it evenly to make a flat-topped heap 6in(30cm) deep. Pour on the solution through a fine rose at up to 3 gallons (13.6 litres) to 1 square yard (0.8m²), pausing from time to time to stir the heap and to ensure that the whole bulk gets treated. You may find the fumes irritating to the eyes and nose, but they will not harm you.

Cover the heap completely with a polythene sheet to lock in the fumes while they work their way through the soil. Remove the cover after four days and fork the heap daily for a couple of weeks to get it thoroughly aired. The smell should have gone by this time, indicating that the soil is ready to go back into the border, or to be used wherever clean soil is needed.

Swapping Soil

You can save a little of this work – though not as much as you might think – by simply swapping the greenhouse soil for some healthy topsoil from the garden. This involves a great deal of shovelling and barrowing, and there is no certainty of getting rid of every scrap of infected material. If you try it, you would still be wiser to switch to another crop which is less susceptible, to reduce the danger of a quick fresh build-up of the soil infection. If you are particularly anxious to continue growing the same subject, you should consider growing it in pots or other containers instead of in the open soil of the border. Pots and containers call for a different type of soil, as explained later.

In swapping infected border soil, it is important to remember a general rule for handling any infected material, that is, to keep it clear of clean material. First, the infected soil should be dug out and wheeled to a spot near where it is to be spread later but clear of the soil which is to be wheeled in. When removal is complete the border and tools should be disinfected. Not till then should the new soil be wheeled in. Apart from the general risk of soil sickness or soil infection, some greenhouse subjects which are popular with the amateur are prone to a crippling disease, verticillium wilt, which infects the soil. It is caused by a fungus and may be imported on seedling plants; so there is a risk when buying plants, as the majority of growers do, of starting serious trouble in your soil, if you plant direct into the border. The fungus will infect soil in outdoor conditions too, so whether plants are for growing indoors or out, care should be taken in the choice of source of supply.

POT SOIL

All greenhouse gardeners use seed-boxes, pots and other containers for some subjects – many do all their greenhouse gardening that way. In such cases it is common to cement all or part of the floor, on the basis that the soil is not wanted. This is a mistake, because an earth floor is more friendly to the atmosphere, being able to breathe naturally and help to control the degree of moisture in the air. So soil, even when not being planted, still remains important – but by all means lay a cement pathway, as this will not have any adverse effects.

The soil or root medium we use in pots and containers has to attempt to provide as much as possible of what the plant roots would obtain in the more natural environment of the open garden. Before deciding what soil to put into your pots, it is worth looking at the history of the subject. In the earliest days of glazed structures, when the pots were always called 'flower-pots', soil straight from the garden was tried, but it was soon realised that potted plants needed something more or something different. Gardeners started experimenting with drainage, feeding and watering, to improve the performance of plants in pots. Head gardeners in country houses and stately homes competed to out-do one another when their masters started comparing results in their own gardens with those in establishments which they visited for those weekend, country house parties. An air of secrecy soon grew up, with each head gardener concocting his own soil mixtures. The cult gave us the phrase 'muck and mystery' – a reference to the strange fertiliser ingredients used and the refusal of the gardeners to reveal them or the ratios in which they were mixed. It was all rather unscientific, and much of it was hit-or-miss.

The amateur in those days would gather leaf-mould from the woods and hedgerows and mix it in varying quantities. He would also use grit and coarse sand in quantities varying according to his judgement. More scientific professional gardeners studied the soil composition and made calculated mixtures. Even last century they were using stacked turves to produce loam, which was the soil constituent in potting mixtures.

In an old notebook of mine I have some soil 'recipes', which have been handed down from the 1870s. They show that almost every subject was then reckoned to need its own special soil mixture. The chrysanthemum mix was simply equal parts of loam, leaf-mould and silver sand. No manure is mentioned there, but the plants were prescribed liquid manure 'every third morning'. This was made by stirring a 'spadeful of rotten stable dung' into six gallons of water, allowing it to settle, and then using the clear liquid.

In the same notes, I record the mixture for geraniums as two-thirds loam and one-third 'stable dung beginning to go mouldy'. If this mixture should turn out too stiff, I was to mix in just enough peat (or silver sand) to 'open the pores a trifle'.

The John Innes Breakthrough

The biggest breakthrough in the field of potting and seed-sowing composts came with the scientifically-based John Innes soil composts. They revolutionised soil formulae for plants grown in pots or other containers indoors. When John Innes, a City of London man of property, died in 1904, he left his fortune to be used in experiments and research for the benefit of horticulture. Hence was founded the John Innes Horticultural Research Institute at Merton, Surrey (now at Norwich).

In the 1930s the Institute, under its curator W. J. C. Lawrence and one of his chief assistants, John Newell, gave us the compost recipes which amazed gardeners and destroyed the theory that it was necessary to have a different soil mixture for each subject. Already, by the time the Institute was set up, experiments had suggested that various mixtures of loam, leaf-mould and sand gave the best physical base for a potting compost. But loam is too vague a definition, since different samples can vary as widely as sand and clay. Leaf-mould is equally variable, and sand can range from fine and soft to coarse and flinty. So each of these three constituents was analysed and the three together were tested in varying proportions.

Lawrence and Newell's experiments caused them to specify 'sterilised, moderately heavy loam'. This loam is produced by stacking thick turves from a clay-based soil, grass side down, for six to twelve months and then riddling them through a three-eighths-inch sieve. Such loam is rich in grass roots and other fibres but may contain harmful bacteria and pests, hence it has to be heat-treated to kill pests and diseases. Heating is done by driving steam through the dry soil to heat it rapidly and completely to a temperature just below the boiling point (212^0F or 100^0C) of water. The heating does cause a small chemical change in the soil, enough to make it injurious to plants for a time, but this effect is corrected by the addition of superphosphate, which is part of the base fertiliser as specified on page 43. The next ingredient, leaf-mould, was soon found to be too variable and was dropped in favour of peat. The peat prescribed is 'dust-free moss or sedge peat, only partly decomposed, and moderately coarse in texture'.

Sand too was clearly defined as 'coarse, clean sand containing particles up to an eighth of an inch in diameter'. This is normally found as silver sand. Notice how precise the John Innes Institute was in its specification of the three main physical ingredients. These specifications were the results of literally thousands of carefully recorded experiments and it was this thoroughness that ensured their success in producing one simple physical mixture (plus a base fertiliser) to accommodate all plants. They named three potting composts, which they called Nos 1, 2 and 3, but all are physically the same. The only difference is in the quantities of fertiliser incorporated in them. No. 1, prescribed for general use, contains the standard amount of fertiliser while Nos 2 and 3 incorporate larger measures of the fertiliser, mainly for use in large pots at different stages of growth. At the same time, the Institute produced a formula for a seed–sowing compost.

The secret of the success of these soil mixtures lies in their universal application, which created a huge demand from the moment they were launched. Unfortunately such a demand soon revealed a shortage of one vital ingredient, the soil element. It was not too difficult to find enough peat and sand of the right specification, but the right loam was not always available. To meet the great demand, other loams were used, some sadly lacking in the clay element, but the compost was still such an improvement on previous potting mixtures that the poorer quality of the loam escaped notice for quite a time.

Everyone wanted the composts, and all manner of suppliers started mixing them, including some who were not too scrupulous. Everyone was free to mix his own, and sell what he had to spare, because there was no registered trade mark and the specifications were freely published for all to copy. These potting compost specifications were (parts by volume):

7 parts sterilised loam
3 parts peat
2 parts sand

These ingredients should be measured by what is termed loose bulk, each one being scooped up naturally into the measure and not packed down. The peat should not be wet but should first have been moistened by putting it in a bucket or other container with a little water in the bottom and leaving it overnight to soak up what it needs. (Note that it is best to put the water in first.) When the peat is properly moistened, it can be squeezed in the hand without causing water to run out.

To each bushel (8 gallons or 36.4 litres) of the compost you should add ¾oz(20g) of ground limestone or chalk (calcium carbonate) and mix it in well. For No. 1 Potting Compost (usually referred to as JIP 1) you should then add 4oz(100g) of the John Innes Base Fertiliser to each bushel. For No. 2 Potting Compost (JIP 2) the measure of base fertiliser is 8oz(225g) to the bushel. For No. 3 Potting Compost (JIP 3) the measure of base fertiliser is 12oz(350g) to the bushel.

The richer composts are designed to support strong growing plants, and as a general guide JIP 1 is rich enough for plants in pots up to 5in(12cm); JIP 2 for pots up to 8in(20cm); and JIP 3 for anything larger. Bear in mind that this fertiliser is an essential basic enrichment only and does not rule out the extra feeding given to many plants during their season of active growth. John

Innes Base Fertiliser is available from garden centres and shops. If you mix your own, note that unlike the loam, peat and sand, the ingredients are measured by weight. The formula is:

2lb(900g) superphosphate
2lb(900g) hoof and horn meal
1lb(450g) sulphate of potash

Mix these together throughly before using at the rates stated above.

The John Innes Seed Compost uses ingredients similar to those in the potting composts but in different proportions and without the basic fertiliser. The mixture is:

2 parts loam
1 part peat
1 part coarse sand

Put it through a quarter-inch sieve, and to each bushel add 1½oz (35g) of superphosphate and ¾oz(20g) of ground limestone or chalk.

SOIL-LESS COMPOSTS

In dealing with the subject of soil, we cannot ignore soil substitutes, like peat-based composts, for potting and seed-raising. The discovery by the peat suppliers that peat alone made a good basis for potting and seed composts came at a time when the John Innes composts were going through a bad patch due to the loam problems. Some excellent peat composts soon flooded the market, with the result that the demand for John Innes composts fell drastically.

Manufacturers of peat composts naturally do not tell us their precise formula so we cannot copy them, but they are readily available in various sizes of pack and also as pillow-sized growing-bags which can be used without normal containers. After some years of competition in which peat took over the lion's share of the market, the John Innes Manufacturers Association, whose members are pledged to stick strictly to the

Institute's correct formula, got together and registered their
'Seal of Approval' for compost containing the right ingredients,
correctly mixed. This guarantee revived the fortunes of the
famous soil-based composts, which many people prefer as
being more natural.

The domestic gardener, with potted plants to look after, now
has a fair choice. He can rely on either soil-based or soil-less
composts to give him good results, so he can choose according
to whatever factors concern him most.

Soil or Peat?

From a purely physical point of view, peat composts are
considered by some people to be clean to handle because there
is nothing sticky in them. In the dry state, they can be rubbed
off the hands as simply as blowing away dust. This characteris-
tic is a disadvantage to those who have to leave plants un-
attended for any length of time during active growth, and to
busy people generally, because peat can be a menace if it goes
dry. If you have a pot plant growing in a peat compost and you
let it go too dry, you will find that it will just float out of its pot
when you try to give it water. Even if you took the plant, pot
and all, and plunged them into a bucket of water, they would at
first float awkwardly, with the plant lying on its side, like debris
washed up by the sea.

The fact is that dry peat is almost impossible to re-wet except
by immersion, hence the correct procedure for moistening peat
is first to put the water into the bucket, then to put the peat on
the surface of the water and leave it. The peat must be left to
take up water gradually, in its own time.

Your over-dry plant could fail to recover, but that is not to say
it would have fared much better in a soil compost. The
difference is that soil is easier to re-wet, and, assuming the
dryness was not fatal, filling the pot saucer with water would be
effective with a soil compost, whereas a peat compost would
bob about and need extra attention. If you rely on peat
composts, therefore, you must be more meticulous in your
attention to watering.

The light weight of peat composts has another disadvantage,
in that plants can so easily become top-heavy and unstable.

Away from these factors, the difference between soil and peat is that soil is a living medium, full of the bacteria which is so important in natural root development. This is something that appeals to many keen gardeners, such as those who specialise in a pet subject for exhibition. Even so, there is nothing about peat to offend enthusiasts in organic gardening. Generally, what we seek in a soil for use in the restricted environment of the plant-pot is a medium that is well balanced regarding moisture-holding capacity, and 'open' enough to breathe freely. And that, of course, is achieved in the specification devised by the John Innes Institute.

THE GARDEN FRAME

The garden frame means different things to different people. As its name indicates, it is a frame – something with four sides. These sides are, to the small area they enclose, as a fence is to a garden in that they keep off draughts and cold winds. This makes them a useful shelter for tender plants whether planted in the ground, enclosed or in containers. Plants in pots, boxes and other containers can benefit from this, and from further protection provided by a 'light', which is a glazed cover. In such situations, the same soil factors apply as in the greenhouse.

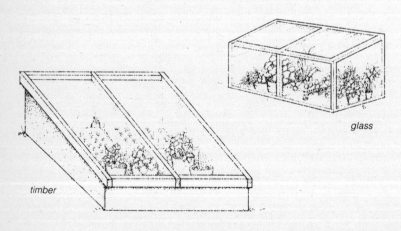

Fig 19   Garden frames.

Where plants are set directly in the soil, the rules are similar to those for the greenhouse border, except that a change of soil is not so likely to be needed. This is partly because the most popular types of plant grown (lettuce, for example) would not cause soil problems. Where a soil change does become necessary, perhaps after growing melons, the change is easily achieved by lifting the frame to a fresh site.

The garden frame is sometimes used for what is called a hotbed, which is a soil-warming trick done with a heap of manure. The manure is topped by a thick layer of soil, and the frame, with its cover, is placed on top. The steamy, heated environment suits cucumbers, and is an excellent idea where the greenhouse is wanted for plants which like a more buoyant atmosphere. At the end of the season, the frame can be re-sited and the hotbed material dug out to help improve the soil in another part of the garden.

7
Pests and Diseases

Soil is a living thing, far removed from any concept of inert dust or dirt. Besides being alive itself, soil is full of matter which supports both plant life and animal life, and also contains a fascinating collection of creatures, all of which are important to the soil itself, to the plants which it supports, to gardeners and to all of us as consumers of what it produces.

Man, being the superior animal, considers himself more important than any other animal or any other form of life. His attitude towards animals and insects is that if they please him they may be classified as 'good'. If they irritate, annoy him or get in the way of his plants, he will classify them as 'bad' and possibly attempt to eliminate them. He may understand the earthworm and accept that it is good for the soil, but when it leaves its casts all over his lawn he wants rid of it quickly. All this is rather arrogant, but it stems from a commendable desire to improve the quality and quantity of what the soil produces, and to beautify the environment.

The term pest is defined as a troublesome, annoying or destructive thing. On that basis, the worm in the lawn is sometimes listed as a pest, simply because its casts are annoying. Good gardeners, however, would deplore its destruction. As gardeners, we like to distinguish between those things which are merely troublesome or annoying, and those which are destructive. Hence, when we refer to an animal or insect as a garden pest, we are classing it as a creature which reduces the quality or quantity of what the soil produces. On that basis, a creature sometimes may be a pet and sometimes a pest. The rabbit is a pet until he escapes and eats your row of lettuces; the deer is a beautiful creature until he eats the young buds off the rose bushes; birds are friends until one pecks the buds from the polyanthuses.

We as superior animals should learn to judge little creatures fairly and forgive them their trespasses. We ought to be able to protect our plants and deter those creatures which annoy, rather than hunting and killing them. Where possible, try to remove what is attracting the pest, rather than attack the pest itself. Take, for instance, the little grey wood-louse. This creature operates by night and is not seen much by day until you turn over a stone or other piece of debris. It feeds chiefly on rotting material such as old timber. I have never had trouble with it, though it is reputed to damage the roots, stems and leaves of some plants, particularly tomatoes and cucumbers, in timber or part-timber greenhouses. The wood of such greenhouses should be treated with one of the modern wood preservatives, such as Bio Woody, which is a fungicide and is harmless to plants. I have always found that if all loose debris, including bricks, stones, old boxes, bits of wood, and dead plant material is cleared away, the wood-lice disappear. If you have plants which are being attacked despite the action I have described, you can treat the soil with Gamma-HCH, or another insecticide of a similar strength.

Whatever action we feel is necessary against pests, we should not only distinguish between friend and foe but should try to avoid harming friendly creatures accidentally. Systemic insecticides applied when plants are clear of insects will affect aphids which later suck the sap, but will not harm our friends the bees and ladybirds. If insecticides are likely to fall on open blooms, apply them only at dusk after the birds have gone to bed.

COMMON GARDEN PESTS

Bean Seedfly

By the time this pest has made his attack it is too late to repair the damage. Its maggot eats into the germinating seeds of all kinds of beans, and sometimes peas. Usually the gardener does not realise the problem until he starts probing in the soil to find out why the seed seems so slow to germinate. Sometimes damaged seedlings send up shoots but these either wilt quickly or are seen to be distorted. Placing Bromophos in the seed drill at sowing time will prevent attacks.

Bulb Mite

This tiny creature, which is often present in the soil, exploits injury or damage done to bulbs either mechanically or by other pests such as eelworms. There is not much one can do about it when the bulb is in the ground. A hot water treatment before planting is useful, but is not practical for the amateur. The best answer is to avoid the initial damage.

Bulb Scale Mite

This is smaller than the bulb mite and is equally difficult to control without a hot water treatment. It breeds inside the bulb, and its presence is indicated by the rust-coloured streaks it causes on the leaves. The flowers will also be blemished.

Cabbage Root Fly

The fly lays its eggs in the soil close to any of the brassica plants, mostly during April and May. When the maggots hatch out, they start feeding on the fibrous roots. The clear sign of damage is a wilting of the leaves due to lack of root sustenance. If a plant is pulled out of the soil the root will be found to be bare. The pest does a vast amount of damage and will quickly work right through a row of seedlings.

Since the fly likes to lay her eggs close up to the plant, deterrents are sometimes used (such as tarred discs) to put the fly off the scent, and other subjects are often planted close by to confuse the fly. Crop rotation is important and soil insecticides such as Bromophos, applied when transplanting, are usually effective.

Capsid Bugs

There are several types of these little insects, which do serious damage to the leaves and shoots of fruits, chrysanthemums, and several other plants. Clean soil cultivation can help to control them, because they overwinter in plant debris on the surface. Soil around vulnerable plants can be treated with HCH or other soil insecticide. Infested plants can be sprayed with systemic insecticides.

Carrot Fly

The pupae of this pest overwinter in the soil near where the previous year's crop was grown. They emerge as flies in June, when they lay their eggs in the soil near carrots and parsnips. The eggs hatch into maggots which do considerable damage as they eat into the roots. Handling the crop during thinning releases the scent which attracts the fly, so this handling should be kept to the minimum. Clean and thorough cultivation of the soil is the best weapon against this pest. Infested plants and debris should be destroyed in autumn.

Chafer Beetles

There are several of these, and all are serious pests – the large cock-chafer, the summer chafer, the garden chafer and the rose chafer. Although the beetles damage a wide range of plants, the most serious damage is that done by the grubs, which live in the soil and attack roots, bulbs and tubers. The grubs are white, with distinct brown heads. This is another pest calling for good clean cultivation of the soil to expose the grubs and help birds to find them.

Chrysanthemum Stool Miner

Small maggots tunnel into the roots of chrysanthemums throughout the summer, inhibiting the production of basal shoots. Soil infestation can be controlled by HCH, and this same insecticide can be used in solution to treat roots which have become infested.

Codling Moth

The maggot of this pest feeds on the cores of apples and pears and does not become a soil problem unless infested apples fall and are left on the ground. It is therefore important to gather up fallen fruits promptly and destroy them. Above ground, the treatment is to apply two or three sprays of a suitable insecticide, such as Fenitrothion, beginning in mid-June.

Cutworm

Several species of this pest inhabit soil near the surface. They are grey-brown, fat caterpillars and they feed at night on the leaves and stems of vegetables and herbaceous plants. Although they chew both roots and stems, their most devastating trick is to cut right through stems at ground level. Soil should be kept loose,, and clear of weeds, to help the birds, but where serious attacks occur Bromophos can be raked in.

Earwig

This is another character which does not inhabit the soil but takes advantage when leaves and debris are left on the surface. It is a night feeder and hides during the day, when it can be found if litter is stirred or plants shaken. Dusting the ground close to plants with HCH will deter the insects.

Eelworm

This thin, near-transparent creature, which looks like a miniature eel, is so microscopic that millions could be active in one infested narcissus bulb. Other bulbs, and several herbaceous plants (including potato and tomato) are subject to attacks by species of eelworm. The only effective remedy is to destroy infected plants and *not* to replace them, because the pest remains in the soil for years. One species, root-knot eelworm, attacks the roots of greenhouse plants. It is difficult to detect any type of eelworm, simply because of their size. Plants affected look sick and fail to develop properly, but the speed of plant reactions varies.

Potato Cyst Eelworm

This can be diagnosed with the help of a magnifying glass which may reveal tiny, round, yellow or brown cysts on the roots of plants which have collapsed. Each cyst may contain several hundred eggs too small to be seen without a powerful microscope.

Clean cultivation is the best hope of avoiding soil infection by any of these destructive pests, but it is also important to buy only top-class plant material, to get it from a reliable source, to practise crop rotation in the vegetable garden, and to use sterilised soil in greenhouses.

Gall Wasp

The larvae of nearly all species of this wasp produce galls on the roots of oak trees, besides those galls seen above ground. The harm they do to soil and garden plants is not significant enough to warrant any chemical treatment.

Leaf-Cutter Bee

These insects make their nests in the soil and the only visible sign is a small hole in the ground. Some nests are found in old brickwork. The bees look like small, hairy, hive bees and they give away their nest positions when they fly in and out with the tiny semi-circular pieces of leaf which they use to make their breeding cells. Although they disfigure the leaves of roses, and other shrubby plants, the damage is not usually serious. Heavy attacks will weaken young plants, however, and where action is deemed necessary the answer is to dig out and destroy the nests at dusk.

Leatherjacket

Crane-flies (daddy-long-legs) are the parents of this pest which lives in the soil, feeding on the roots of both flowering and vegetable plants. It is a greyish-brown grub, which is soft but has a tough skin. It is extremely damaging in lawns, where it kills patches of grass by chewing off the whole root system, before its presence is noticed. In the flower garden, it eats its way into bulbs and in bad cases kills them. Similarly, in the vegetable garden it tunnels its way into roots. Moist ground suits it best and it will be found in menacingly large numbers after a wet winter. It does not like sandy soil, particularly in a drought.

Gardens made on newly-dug grassland usually have a big population of this pest and chemical control is not favoured because an effective chemical would persist too long in the soil.

Frequent, deep cultivation helps to reduce the numbers, but that is not possible on lawns. An effective lawn treatment is to soak the ground thoroughly and then cover it with black plastic sheeting. When the sheet is lifted early next morning, the grubs will be found on the surface where they can be left to the birds, or swept up. Starlings flying in flocks will sometimes invade gardens and clear the lawn of all the leatherjackets they can find in a systematic search.

Millepede

Many people confuse this soil pest with the beneficial insect, the centipede. A simple rule I was taught as a boy was, 'If it runs away at speed, it is a friend; if it moves slowly it is a pest.' The swift mover is the centipede, and the slower character, which tends to curl up when disturbed, is the millepede. There are various types, some black and some spotted, and all do considerable damage to the roots of many plants. One lazy habit of theirs is to exploit damage done by other pests or diseases if they can find any. They feed in ready-made holes or on roots already softened by disease, so when millepedes are found, checks should be made to see whether other pests, possibly slugs and wireworms, are present. They also infest bulbs and tubers (including potatoes).

Where possible, control should be attempted by cultivation, rather than by the use of chemicals. But where chemicals are needed, Slug Gard by PBI helps control slugs, leatherjackets, wireworms, as well as millepedes.

Narcissus Fly

Bulbs infested by the maggot of this fly will fail to flower, will make few leaves and will go soft. Such bulbs must not be left in the soil but should be detected as early as possible and destroyed. At planting time, any bulb found to be soft should be destroyed – cutting it open would reveal probably a lone, fat maggot. The fly lays its eggs during May and June in the hole left in the soil surface where the foliage has died down. To reduce risk, keep the bulbs fully covered by soil throughout this time.

Slug and Snail

In the soil, the slug does serious damage, and will ruin a potato crop, without detection until it is too late. Although it is a night-time feeder, surface activity can be spotted by the trails of slime made by the pest as it moves. In the flower garden, the young shoots of delphinium are a favourite target, but nothing escapes this pest's attention. Damp soil is most affected, especially if not regularly stirred by cultivation, which is an important safeguard. There are various chemical remedies on the market, but the snail is a less serious pest and is easy to capture. Plant debris, stones and other litter, especially in damp corners, should be checked frequently for slugs and snails hiding under them.

Swift Moth Caterpillar

This dirty-white creature has a brownish head, and can grow up to 2in(5cm) long. It feeds on bulbs, gladioli corms, and the roots of herbaceous plants and weeds, particularly docks and nettles. Good cultivation and weed control reduce the risk of attack, but where the presence of the pest is suspected, Bromophos should be raked into the soil before planting.

Weevil

There are several species of weevil which damage plants, and the white grub of the vine weevil is probably the worst. Like other soil pests it works unseen, and fatal damage is done to roots before warning signs appear. If a small rockery plant collapses and dies, a search of the soil will probably reveal the grub, if it hasn't already moved on to another root. With pot plants, a change of soil and the treatment of the new soil with HCH is the remedy where practical. But the trouble most often occurs when the plant is in full growth and cannot withstand a complete change of soil on top of the suffering already caused by the grub. In that event the roots should be searched carefully, the grubs picked out, and the soil soaked in HCH solution at normal spray strength.

Wireworm

Grassland soil will almost certainly contain this shiny, yellow-brown grub, which is the larva of the click beetle; where grassland is turned over to potatoes, the tubers will probably be ruined by its tunnelling. In gardens newly dug from grassland, a potato planted in the soil will help attract the pest away from valuable plants. For this trick to be effective, the potato should be on a stick and should be taken up each morning for invading grubs to be removed. Search and destroy is still the best treatment – this, with the help given by birds, normally gets rid of the problem in two or three seasons. Meanwhile Bromophos should be raked in before a vulnerable crop is sown or planted.

SOIL-BORNE DISEASES

Most of the diseases found in the soil come from sick or damaged plants, and in good gardening practice such plants are removed speedily and completely to avoid soil contamination. Even where disease starts from soil-borne bacteria, clean cultivation will limit the damage and restrict its spread.

Some soil problems remain a mystery. With rose sickness, for instance, the soil in a well established rose-bed inexplicably refuses to nourish a healthy new rose bush, despite all routine efforts. The ultimate answer is to make a new rose-bed on a fresh site. Whatever subject is being grown, it is always wise to make changes rather than to keep on growing the same subject on the same site. Such changes (essential with most vegetables) prevent a steady build-up of any pest or disease to which the species is prone. Good husbandry involves being able to recognise a sick plant. The following are some of the more common soil diseases.

Club Root

The name describes the club-like appearance of the swollen, foul-smelling root typical of a cabbage plant infested by the fungus *Plasmodiophora brassica*.

Brassicas are the principal but not the only plants attacked by the fungus. In the flower garden, it may strike wallflowers and stocks. It thrives in badly-drained, acid soil and, if those conditions are avoided, the chief risk of infection is in bringing in infected plants. Such plants are unlikely to come from commercial sources, rather they usually come from friends whose hitherto healthy garden has just become infested and who have not detected it. You must therefore exercise caution when plant gifts are offered, since the disease is extremely difficult to deal with. Where there is suspicion of club root infestation in the soil, no susceptible subject should be planted until the soil has been proved safe.

People who wish to grow plants of the cabbage family on suspect land are known to risk it after certain precautions, rather than wait years to get rid of the fungus. They lime the soil heavily ½lb(225g) hydrated lime to 1 square yard (0.8m^2) – put calomel dust on seed-beds and in the planting holes, harvest the vegetables while they are young, and practise strict rotation of crops. This is a crisis effort and not one to be recommended because it does not get rid of the problem.

Crown Rot

When this occurs in rhubarb the plants should be destroyed and any replacement should go on to a fresh site. Although the bacteria is soil-borne, it usually attacks where the crown has been damaged. Where such damage is avoided and the soil is well drained, there is not much danger of an attack.

Damping-Off

Seedlings growing in boxes under glass can look healthy one day and yet the next day a small percentage will have fallen over and the stem at ground level will be seen to have withered to a thin brown thread. This is due to a parasitic fungus which lives on dead and decaying matter in the soil. The rot is started by bruising tiny seedlings during pricking-out just after germination. The remedy is to water the box of seedlings with a solution of Cheshunt Compound, which is a mixture of finely-powdered copper sulphate and ammonium carbonate. But this remedy needs to be applied immediately because the rot spreads rapidly. The trouble can be avoided by using sterilised soil, avoiding over-watering or high temperatures, and by handling seedlings tenderly.

Honey Fungus

Also known as bootlace fungus, this is probably the worst of the soil-borne diseases, since it may attack almost any plant root. Privet is one of its best-known victims in the garden but hardly anything is immune and so no risk should be taken.

The fungus (*Armillaria mellea*) lives on dead, woody roots, especially on wet, badly-drained soil. Usually it manifests itself first on a piece of root left in the ground after an unwanted tree or shrub has been removed. Cutting down a tree and leaving the stump to rot is always a risk. When digging out a stump, it is not enough to remove most of the root – any bits left in the soil are liable to become infected. The fungus develops 'bootlaces' which spread in all directions and invade any root they reach. Surface evidence of the fungus takes the form of a cluster of honey-coloured toadstools.

Soil in which infected plants have been found should be soaked with a solution of sulphate of iron at 4oz(100g) to the gallon (4.5 litres).

Powdery Scab

The fungus responsible for this trouble, also known as corky scab of potatoes, attacks tomatoes too and is difficult to eradicate from the soil. On the potato tuber, it forms a scab which bursts to scatter a brown powder of disease spores. The treatment is to burn all infected plant material and to practise strict rotation of crops in the vegetable garden.

Tulip Fire

Infected bulbs have small black fungal growths easily visible on the outer scales, while leaves and flowers are damaged, and a grey mould is also seen. This is a serious disease, and one which is difficult to treat – any infected bulb should be destroyed immediately by burning. Healthy bulbs lifted from the same bed should be treated with suspicion. Dip them in benomyl, isolate them in store, and during storage discard any that show signs of softening. Dip the bulbs again before planting. Treat the soil with the same fungicide and do not replant it with bulbs.

Wart Disease

Fortunately, this soil-borne disease of potatoes is no longer common as immunity has been bred into modern varieties of seed potato – but action must be taken whenever it is suspected. Infected soil must not be planted and where infection occurs the Ministry of Agriculture *must*, by law, be informed immediately. The disease is caused by a fungus which survives as resting spores in the soil. The fungus attacks swelling tubers, causing large warts to appear on the skin. These warts produce more resting spores which keep the soil infected. There is no chemical cure and all suspect tubers should be destroyed.

Wilt

Two wilt diseases caused by soil-borne fungi are fusarium wilt and verticillium wilt. The first attacks mainly dwarf and runner beans, peas and dianthus. Drooping, stunted plants with yellowing leaves will be found to have reddish-brown streaks inside their stems. There is no cure, and infected plants should be put into the incinerator. The soil should be sterilised and given a change of crop. Verticillium wilt also attacks dianthus, besides a number of perennials, shrubs and trees. The obvious indication of the presence of the disease is wilting, but browning of the leaves is another sign. Roots of established plants are less prone to attack than younger ones but wherever the disease strikes, the answer is usually the same – dig up the plants and burn them. If spotted in time on woody plants, the infected stems can be cut back to healthy growth and the cuts treated with a fungicidal paint.

Index